Crisis! The Taxpayer Revolt And Your Kids' Schools

by Efrem Sigel, Dantia Quirk and
Patricia Whitestone
with Ronald L. Soble

Knowledge Industry Publications, Inc.
White Plains, New York 10604

Crisis! The Taxpayer Revolt and Your Kids' Schools
by
Efrem Sigel, Dantia Quirk and Patricia Whitestone,
with Ronald L. Soble

Library of Congress Catalog Card Number 78-60967
ISBN 0-914236-28-8

Printed in the United States of America

Contents

PREFACE

The idea for this book came the evening after California voted to approve Proposition 13, as the shock of that vote and its implications for education and other public services began to sink in.

The editorial staff at Knowledge Industry Publications enthusiastically agreed to put it together, even though this meant an unprecedented effort at gathering information and at writing under deadline pressure. Ron Soble of the *Los Angeles Times* contributed an account of the Proposition 13 campaign for chapter 2. Other members of the Knowledge Industry Publications staff besides the authors who contributed to the interviewing, writing and editing were Seth Goldstein and Ben Compaine.

During a one-week period our staff interviewed some 100 educators and public officials around the country. While there are too many to list them individually, the authors wish to thank all who cooperated so generously to make this book possible.

This book is dedicated to the 3.3 million children, including my son Jonathan, who start first grade this fall. It was written in the conviction that public education demands public participation, and that information is the critical resource that makes such participation a reality.

E.S.
June 22, 1978

1
Introduction
The Crisis in Education

This fall some 3.3 million children step inside a first grade classroom to begin their formal education.

Whatever region of the country they live in, whether they come from well-to-do homes or poor ones, the emotions of these youngsters will be remarkably similar. Is the teacher mean or nice? Will I be able to find my way home, or down the hall? How do I learn to read? To add and subtract? To tell time?

Even in a society as rich in information and in ways to learn as ours, nothing has yet replaced formal schooling as the process by which new generations are initiated into shared ways of thinking, learning, doing. Crossing the threshold of that first grade classroom is the first step of an initiation as transforming as the rites of passage of any traditional culture.

For the 335,000 first graders residing in the state of California, this September's entry into the classroom is especially poignant. Not since the early days of forced desegregation, some 20 years ago, has such uncertainty surrounded the opening of the public schools. On June 6, 1978, California citizens overwhelmingly approved a state constitutional amendment, the Jarvis-Gann Initiative, limiting property taxes to 1% of market value. The amendment will cut local property taxes from $12 billion to $5 billion almost overnight, reducing total revenue available to the state and localities combined by some 18%, and to localities alone by close to 30%.

The California Teachers Association has urged its members to resist layoffs and salary cuts. Its position is that school districts should refuse to open unless they can provide normal educational services. If they do open, it urges they should operate the schools as before, shutting down entirely when the money runs out.

While the state will make up part of the loss from its current surplus, cities and localities in California are being forced to consider drastic cuts in spending and in the provision of services. What's more, the California experience is already being held up as a model for other states — Oregon, Utah, Michigan, Massachusetts — where high taxes invite voter retaliation and retrenchment.

TAX REVOLT AND EDUCATION

The tax revolt and education stand in uneasy relationship to each other. Thirty eight percent of the state and local taxes collected in the United States go to operate a vast, decentralized system of public schools. No service is more visible, more criticized, more central to the functioning of a democratic society, than public education.

No concept has been the object of more disillusionment in the past decade, as the ideal of schools that would foster social equality and individual betterment confronted the stubborn persistence of inequality, functional illiteracy and rampant unemployment among school dropouts or even school graduates.

The origins of the taxpayer revolt expressed in California's Proposition 13 go far beyond dissatisfaction with education. Other public services have come in for virulent criticism: welfare, notably; police protection and the criminal justice system, to be sure; health and hospital care, sanitation, highways, among others.

There is a strong strain of resentment in the antitax movement against poorer, more dependent members of society: families on welfare, kids who have difficulty learning, college students on government grants and loans, people receiving unemployment checks, perhaps even older people on Medicare or social security. Voters have a perception that more and more of the benefits of government are going to those who can't or won't provide for themselves.

Whether the perception stands up under analysis is less important than the fact that some abuses do exist. With each revelation that *some* welfare recipients cheat, *some* loan recipients have no intention of repaying the government and *some* on unemployment actually are vacationing in Florida during the winter, taxpayers become more cynical about the social purposes of government. Mario Cuomo, a candidate for New York state lieutenant governor, has warned against letting the legitimate anger over high taxes turn into a vendetta against "the poor and politically powerless." Nevertheless, it will be the rare politician who speaks such unpopular words if the antitax movement mushrooms.

Increases in Tax Burden

There is no denying the tax burden that led to the revolt in California and other states. Between 1970 and 1976 general revenue of state and local government increased from $130.8 billion to $256.2 billion, a 96% jump. Tax collections and spending grew at twice the rate of inflation in this period. Property taxes, while declining from 26% to 22% of the total, still zoomed in dollars, from $34 billion to $57 billion. The per capita burden of state and local taxes was

$731 in 1976, but such populous states as New York, California, Michigan and Massachusetts are well above this figure.

Clearly the case can be made for more discipline in public spending at all levels of government. But in what form, and at what speed? A dispassionate view of the consequences of any sudden, massive reduction in local government spending must start with the following assumptions:

• Drastically pruning the revenues available to states and localities entails similar reductions in their outlays.

• Since education is by far the largest element in state and local budgets, the schools will shoulder the burden of cutbacks.

• And since 60 million Americans are either enrolled in or employed by institutions of public education, while another 8 million attend or work in private schools and colleges (altogether, those involved in the educational enterprise come to 32% of the population), any substantial cutbacks in educational expenditures will touch many of the households in the U.S.

The purpose of this book is to lay out as clearly as possible the dimensions of the current taxpayer revolt and its implications for the education of America's children. While the voters in California have spoken, citizens in states accounting for the other 90% of the population have yet to express themselves on similar measures.

It is true that the week of the California vote, voters in scores of Ohio school districts — including Cleveland and Columbus, the state's largest cities — turned down increased tax levies for the schools. A week later voters in various Michigan districts also said no to higher school taxes. But these decisions were still being made on a district by district basis; they did not impose a statewide ceiling on tax collections, as in California. The first test in another state of the mood that led to victory for Proposition 13 was to come in Oregon. There, supporters needed to gather enough signatures by July to put their referendum on the November ballot.

Aftermath of Proposition 13

Even in California, the outcomes of Proposition 13 can not be considered as cast in stone. Court tests are already underway of whether Proposition 13 violates the California and U.S. constitutions — tests initiated by various localities and by the California Teachers Association. Whether the court tests fail or not — and it would have to be a brave panel of judges who would overturn a measure approved by 65% of the electorate — the ultimate fate of Proposition 13 depends on whether voters in succeeding elections agree to let it stand.

Electoral politics is the politics of change. Voters choose one candidate over another, approve or reject a referendum or bond issue having not convictions but perceptions of what their vote entails. Sentiment may triumph over common sense at any given moment, but in managing its affairs, government, like business, cannot operate under illusion for too long before a catastrophe sets in and a correction ensues.

Proponents of Proposition 13 in California contended that catastrophe had indeed arrived in the form of runaway government taxation that soaked up an ever increasing percentage of personal income, choking off personal choice and economic development. They see the vote of June 6 as the required correction. Opponents of the proposition depict the constitutional amendment as the catastrophe, one that will create far greater dislocations in personal choice and economic well being than the taxation it aimed to curb. Clearly one limitation of the referendum approach to budget-cutting is the lack of flexibility it allows for special circumstances.

As long as Proposition 13 was a proposition and not a law, this debate could proceed without the benefit of any practical experience. Now, however, experience will catch up with theory. As this book was being written, localities in California were frantically racing to trim their budgets in order to fit the economic strictures of the amendment. The opinions, perceptions and concrete decisions of those concerned with education are described at length in later chapters of this book.

At this writing, it seems clear that Proposition 13 will not mean the dismantling of the system of public education in California, but it will create dislocations in public service which in some cases will recall the Depression of the 1930s. State aid will reduce the first year impact to perhaps a 10% budget cut, but even so thousands of teachers are certain to lose their jobs. In some districts average class sizes will jump; in other districts it will be held down only by instituting split sessions. Local purchases of supplies and teaching materials are being reduced to an absolute minimum, and any activity of the schools not connected to academic instruction — extracurricular activities, athletics, evening school and summer programs — is being scrutinized or eliminated. For some, these actions mark the logical culmination of an emphasis in American education on back to basics, and on the discarding of so-called frills. For others, they are a perversion of the ideal of an educational system devoted to nurturing each child's abilities and talents.

ORIGINS OF PROPOSITION 13

It was 20 years from the launching of Sputnik to the launching of the campaign to slash the property tax in California; in fact it could be said that the children of Sputnik were the fathers of the tax movement. The generation of students in high school at the time of the first Russian space shot was one of the groups that voted in favor of the amendment. No matter that this group had children of their own in school; they were the most heavily taxed and the most heavily squeezed of any age group in the population.

Between 1957 and 1977, American education has been the recipient of massive investments of public funds. The late 1950s and the entire decade of the 1960s were characterized by rapidly growing educational enrollments, and even more rapidly surging expenditures. Spending on education rose from $21 billion in 1959-60 to $120 billion in 1975-76. Only part of this increase is due to inflation; the fact is that education has taken an ever greater slice of national and personal income. As a percentage of the Gross National Product, education expenditures rose from 4.8% in 1957 to 7.9% in 1975. (In contrast, spending on defense fell from 9.9% of GNP in 1957 to 5.5% in 1975.)

Demands Made on Schools

Throughout the 1960s Americans looked to the schools to solve social problems that now seem unsolvable. Desegregation was a focus for much educational policymaking in that decade, as redistricting, paired schools, open enrollment plans and finally, forced busing were tried in one district after another. Compensatory education was another focus. The passage of the Elementary and Secondary Education Act of 1965, one of the most ambitious of all the "Great Society" programs of President Johnson, ranks as the federal government's most sweeping endeavor to improve the education of poor children, many of whom were black or Spanish-speaking. Other elements of the federal initiatives of the 1960s were federal loans and grants for higher education, and an emphasis on educational innovation at all levels. Head Start and other pre-school programs, use of television and audiovisual media, individualized instruction, ungraded classrooms, the offering of new courses (modern literature, Afro-American studies), work-study programs — all these experiments proliferated. Educators began speaking a new jargon, hired experts whose talents consisted of writing proposals for innovative programs to be funded by one or another bureau of the Department of Health, Education and Welfare.

The flurry of new ideas shook up the educational system, and a bit of ferment in something as traditional as schooling never hurts. But many of the set pieces of educational policy seemed to have no clear basis in fact. The Coleman Report of 1966 found that pupil achievement had much more to do with the background of children than with the resources devoted to their schooling. Evaluations of Title I programs often could identify no apparent gains in the children they served. Head Start did give poor kids a leg up, but by third or fourth grade many had fallen back again. Putting dull lessons on television proved no spur to learning, and investing large sums in computers, teaching machines, or other hardware was no guarantee of stimulation either.

Reaction in 1970s

By the early 1970s, a strong reaction had begun to set in to the educational innovations of the previous decade, which were often derided as misguided social tinkering. Back to basics became a rallying cry in 1974 and 1975. Concern over test scores in reading and math, indications that there were functionally illiterate high school graduates, coupled with continuing parental concern with problems of discipline, have had a number of effects in the current decade: the fall from favor of the "new math" as part of the curriculum, the reinstatement of older literature, grammar and handwriting programs, elimination of mini courses and electives in many high schools and a return to stricter grading and more closely supervised pupil activities.

Both economics and demographics also played a role in the reevaluation of the schools. Enrollments in elementary and secondary schools first fell in 1972, and by 1977 the school-going population was down about 5% from its 1971 peak. The overall numbers mask the sharpness of the decline in the older regions of the country. Population has continued to increase in the South, Southwest and West, whereas many school districts in the East and Midwest have lost 15% to 20% of their enrollments. Yet in almost none of those districts has the school budget been cut. For one thing, inflation has pushed up the cost of everything schools buy. For another, there are high fixed costs built into the educational system. It costs as much to heat a classroom with 18 pupils as one with 23 children. Tenure and seniority have mitigated against large-scale reductions in the professional workforce, except by attrition. The cost of debt service and retirement benefits continues no matter how much enrollments drop.

Nevertheless, the recession of 1974-75 brought a foretaste of the austerity promised by California's Proposition 13. Older cities like New York, Philadelphia and Detroit, experiencing severe budget deficits, reduced teaching staffs by the thousands in the 1975 to 1977 period. Nationwide, education spending dropped to roughly the annual rate of inflation, after more than a decade of outstripping that rate.

The passage of Proposition 13 in California marks a low point in public appreciation of local government services in general, and education in particular. Passage of similar measures in other states could mean a wave of school closings, teacher layoffs, spurts in pupil-teacher ratios and elimination of all educational programs except the narrowly academic. At the same time that voters are reducing direct support for the schools, proposals to allow a tax credit for private school tuition are getting their most serious attention in Congress. (Such a bill passed the House of Representatives in 1978, despite the threat of a Presidential veto.) Proponents of the credits say they would help parents struggling with the burden of paying college tuition and private school bills with after-tax dollars. Allowing the credits, they say, would strengthen the middle class and promote freedom of educational choice. Opponents have a starker vision: tax credits for private schooling will cause further middle class flight from the public schools and contribute to the dismantling of the American system of public education. Moreover, they say, allowing such credits for elementary and secondary education violates the First Amendment, and would inevitably be held to be unconstitutional by the U.S. Supreme Court.

LONG-TERM PROBLEM OF CONFIDENCE

It is easy to be carried away by the fervor of the moment and to cry panic about the future of public education. Scores of interviews conducted for this book in June 1978 show that public officials and educators around the country are not panicking, that the tradition of local control of education tends to insulate the U.S. educational system from national shocks. What is revealed, however, is a long-term problem of confidence in education. In the end, this problem poses as great a threat to the schools as the initiatives now being proposed in dozens of states to put a cap on tax collections. Because the vote of June 6 in California either touched off or gave inspiration to many of these initiatives, the next chapter will consider the origins and meanings of the California decision.

2
The California Revolt

California's Great Taxpayer Revolt of 1978 has become an issue that is stirring the nation.

The focus of the uprising is Proposition 13, an amendment to the state constitution which in the June 6 California gubernatorial primary received a resounding 64.7% voter affirmation. The amendment will set in force a sweeping cut of state property tax revenues from an annual level of $12 billion to $5 billion, a slash which is causing widespread chaos in state and local government as lawmakers attempt to grapple with massive cuts in government services and with teacher and public employee layoffs.

But the message of Proposition 13 is loud and clear: homeowners, at least in California, have had it with soaring property taxes. Or, as one veteran political observer put it: "The electorate got mad as hell at government for not coming to its rescue and decided, for once, to do something about it."

The immediate roots of the 1978 tax revolt go back to 1966 — a year of reform that was supposed to help and protect the California taxpayer. That was the year the state legislature undertook to reform the state's property tax law after scandals rocked four county assessors' offices and eventually sent several assessors to prison. Resulting legislation, which bore the sweeping title "A Bill of Rights for Property Owners," tightened assessment procedures and strengthened the property owner's ability to appeal the assessor's valuation.

ORIGINS OF THE REVOLT

Of all the changes triggered by the law, however, one in particular kindled the flames of the tax revolt of the 1970s. Assessors were required to apply a uniform and publicly announced assessment ratio to each of the state's 58 counties. The ratio is that portion of a property's estimated market value against which the tax rate is applied – the so-called assessed value.

Assessors in California had always calculated values "toward" what a given property would presumably bring on the open market. Their assessments consequently were always some fraction of market value. That was all changed in 1966. Instead of an informal method of setting assessments, the law said there would be a flat assessment ratio of 25% of market value for all property throughout California – a goal reached by 1971.

Thus, in the name of equity and uniformity, Sacramento lawmakers had abolished the county assessor's former latitude to adjust local assessments as he saw fit. Under the old system, the assessor could spare certain areas or certain types of property the pain of sharp hikes in assessments. In plain language, up until 1966, assessors had been artificially holding down tax values of residential property while slapping higher assessments on business property. Whatever the failures of this approach, it did help maintain a low profile for both property taxation and assessors.

For example, following World War II, there was a critical shortage in California housing and, in turn, residential real estate became sharply inflated. Local assessors, in the way of the times, diffused the effect of this inflation on taxes through restraint in raising assessments.

Such action now is illegal, and a state agency, the State Board of Equalization, is charged with ensuring that uniform property assessments are made against which the tax rate is applied.

This meant that assessors no longer could control tax bills; it also meant big trouble for homeowners.

When the 1970s brought its unique combination of a sluggish economy accompanied by rampant inflation, home values skyrocketed and, so, assessments soared, too. Suddenly, Californians were faced with the prospect of homes being reassessed 100% or more from the previous reassessment which meant that property taxes paid to local governments could quickly double, too.

Residential Burden Increased

A shift was taking place in which residential, not commercial property was taking on a greater tax burden. At the same time, social programs in health and welfare, such as Medicaid and its California counterpart, Medi-Cal, contributed to rapidly growing state and local budgets; e.g. between 1969-70 and 1976-77, total state spending rose from $6.3 billion to $12.6 billion.

Also during the early 1970s, the recession brought a virtual halt to home and apartment construction. And in 1972, California voters approved tight controls on new coastal construction, creating premium values for shoreline buildings and lots. These unrelated acts put intense pressure on coastal communities, where the statewide wave of inflated property values hit first and hardest.

As property taxes began to soar, constitutional amendments were proposed to brake both rising taxes and increased government spending. One constitutional amendment of the

1970s to put a lid on government spending and end the tax spiral even had then Gov. Ronald Reagan's backing, but it was defeated at the polls.

In fact, using the initiative process to change the state's Constitution is a feat of no small proportions, according to a recent study from the University of California at Berkeley by Eugene C. Lee.

To be sure, notes Lee, "No other large, urban, industrial state in the country employs both the constitutional amendment initiative (where voters signatures can qualify an issue for the ballot) and the direct statutory initiative (where the legislature can place an item on the ballot.)"

But passing such initiatives and making them stick against court scrutiny is another thing. A total of 148 proposed initiative measures sought voter signatures between 1960 and 1978 in California. Twenty-six of these eventually qualified for the ballot and seven were passed by the voters. But, as the University of California study notes, only one (a railroad anti-featherbedding measure) is still fully in effect.

Even so, ballot propositions are an important part of California political life and have been around since 1911 when Gov. Hiram Johnson instituted them as a way of permitting citizens to go over the heads of the legislature, which he felt was controlled by the Southern Pacific Railroad Co.

Over the years, some of the campaigns have been highly emotional, dealing with issues such as race, development of the coastline, pornography, farm labor and the death penalty. But none have generated the grassroots emotion of Proposition 13.

JARVIS AND PROPOSITION 13

Much of the peculiar nature of the debate over Proposition 13 reflected the personality of its chief sponsor, Howard

Jarvis. For the past 15 years, Jarvis, now 75, has been the outspoken champion of lower property taxes in California. His campaign for Proposition 13 in 1978 made him as well known as any of the candidates running for office in California's June primary.

Jarvis caught the public fancy with a style reflecting the finesse of a professional football linebacker blitzing into an opponent's backfield. His oratorical style was complete with four-letter words and a booming voice that could seemingly be heard in several counties at once. The gist of his message was that the basic American right to own property was endangered by the attempts of what he labelled a bunch of insensitive politicians to take away that right.

The Jarvis Initiative, as it became known after it qualified for the California ballot in December 1977 with 1.2 million signatures (almost three times what it legally needed), was cosponsored by Paul Gann, a retired real estate dealer in the Sacramento area.

Proposition 13 would cut all property taxes, commercial and industrial as well as residential, to 1% of market value. Property appraisals would be rolled back to fiscal 1975-76 market values and allowed to climb only 2% annually until a property was resold. Then it could be reappraised to reflect the current market. A two-thirds majority of registered voters would be required to authorize a local tax increase, and no property tax could be hiked under any circumstance. Under the measure, a two-thirds vote of each legislative house would be required to raise any other taxes (such as income and sales) to fill the revenue gap caused by the Jarvis Initiative. (Under the pre-Proposition 13 law, taxes could be increased by the legislature through a simple majority vote.)

Proposition 13's effective date was July 1, 1978.

The campaign to pass Proposition 13 came as the legislature was badly tangled in efforts to pass its own version of property tax reform. A major tax reform package fell apart in 1977 and new efforts at reform in 1978 had been dumped or gotten snarled.

Finally, in March, the Democratic-controlled legislature approved legislation sponsored by state Sen. Peter Behr, a San Rafael Republican who had announced his retirement at the end of the year. The bill would have amended the state constitution in the form of Proposition 8 on the June 6 primary ballot.

Proposition 8: An Alternative

Proposition 8 (Behr) would have cut taxes on all owner-occupied homes by at least 30%. Additional cuts would have been forced by imposing limits on the rate at which property taxes would increase. Under the Jarvis approach, the big tax reduction would apply to commercial and industrial real estate as well as residential; but under Behr, for the first time, owner-occupied residential property could be taxed at a lower rate than commercial and industrial property through a tax roll split provided by the measure. Proposition 8 also increased the state's income tax credit for renters from $37 to $75 while Proposition 13 did nothing for renters. Under Proposition 8, the immediate tax cut on a $60,000 home, for example, would have been $451. But under Proposition 13, it would be $765.

The following table shows what an average California homeowner could have expected in property tax relief from Proposition 8 and what he should get under Proposition 13.

The Behr bill had another strike against it. The legislation was seemingly complex while Jarvis kept his proposal and arguments relatively simple. For example, few voters seemed to understand that the Behr bill would reduce taxes by $1.4

TABLE 2-1
PROPERTY TAX RELIEF
UNDER PROPOSITIONS 8 AND 13

Home Value	Current Tax	Prop. 8 Relief	Prop. 13 Relief
$ 30,000	$ 617	$ 196	$ 329
$ 40,000	$ 885	$ 281	$ 476
$ 50,000	$1,153	$ 365	$ 615
$ 60,000	$1,422	$ 451	$ 765
$ 80,000	$1,958	$ 621	$1,053
$100,000	$2,495	$ 791	$1,333
$200,000	$5,117	$1,581	$2,705

billion without any reduction in current services. The reason is that the reduction could be entirely financed out of the state's bulging budget surplus which by mid-1978 exceeded $5 billion. Also not well understood was a key component in the Behr bill which said that hikes in local property tax revenues would be limited to the rate of increase in the Consumer Price Index; thus the maximum increase for 1978 would be set at 6.5%. Since property values have been rising faster than 6.5% annually, this provision would have tended to force down tax rates.

Finally, a major blow to the success of the Behr bill, or Proposition 8, was the fact that it wasn't signed into law by Gov. Brown until March, about a month after the primary ballots and the voter pamphlet explaining 1978's 13 propositions had gone to press.

Naturally, Proposition 13, which qualified for the ballot in December, had a full explanation in the pamphlet which went out to the state's almost 10 million voters. But the language in the pamphlet describing Proposition 8 was vague, saying only that property tax restrictions depended on the exact form of the legislation to be passed. To be sure, media attention on the two measures was intense, but still, the lack of a ballot explanation for Proposition 8 was seen by its supporters as a big handicap.

CAMPAIGN ON THE PROPOSITIONS

The campaign was as dramatic as any political combat California has seen for years.

Opponents of Proposition 13 declared its $7 billion, or 60%, cut in property tax revenues would play havoc with keeping school personnel at current levels and would cripple many of the state's fire, lighting, sewage and other special districts which are heavily dependent on the property tax for financing.

California's 1042 school districts, for example, are on average, dependent on the property tax for 60% of their financing while the remaining 40% comes from the state. Some fire districts got 80% or more of their funds from the property tax.

Even before the June 6 vote, about 125 of the state's school districts sent layoff notices to teachers. Notices are required by March 15 under California law if teachers are not to be rehired for the following school year. The more than 900 districts that did not send notices now face the prospect (should the courts allow Proposition 13 to stand) that they will have to employ those teachers for the full 1978-79 academic year and hope that the state legislature will bail them out. Chapter 3 discusses how various districts, including the Los Angeles city school district, the state's largest, handled the issue of layoffs.

Jarvis' position during the campaign was that the ax has to fall on some heads if property taxes are to drop and government fat is to be trimmed. For openers, Jarvis doesn't believe that the property tax has to be the financial backbone of the state's school system. Moreover, he said during the campaign, the property tax should "only pay for property-related services. That includes police protection, fire protection, sewer systems, streets, lights, garbage and those things. It should not pay for welfare, food stamps, illegal aliens. The whole gamut shouldn't be on the back of the property owner like it is today."

Jarvis was raised in a Mormon family in Utah but didn't practice the religion. "I was the black sheep," he recalls. He was a Utah newspaper publisher, moving to California in 1934 to begin a successful career as an industrialist. He is still the black sheep as far as most California politicians, big business, public employees, school teachers, organized labor and others who opposed him are concerned.

"We have the people's amendment," Jarvis would bellow to audience after audience in rural and urban areas. He felt he had touched a responsive chord among the electorate that went beyond the property tax issue. The people, he firmly believes, are fed up with government that is insensitive to their needs. "This is the first time since the Boston Tea Party that we have a chance to vote for ourselves for once," he said in underscoring this concept during the campaign.

Such polemics were well thought out by a man who has been active in campaigns for Republican White House candidates from Herbert Hoover to Richard Nixon. "I play on every emotion I can," said Jarvis in a candid interview with a Los Angeles Times reporter. One of these emotions, he said, is the use of the fear technique.

Ironically, one of Jarvis' most strident campaign complaints about the tactics of his opponents was the use of the fear theme in arguments they made that Proposition 13 would curtail police and fire services and reduce the quality of education by eliminating thousands of teachers.

"Mine is legitimate fear," said Jarvis. "The fear of losing property." Thus he stated, "We should have the guts to let the elderly keep their homes" charging that more and more senior citizens on fixed incomes were being forced out of their homes because of soaring property taxes. The campaign for Proposition 13 also drew sustenance from the difficulty middle income groups have in meeting their property tax bills, and the negative impact soaring taxes have on the ability of younger people to purchase their first home.

"One human right above all other rights is the right to own property," Jarvis told one luncheon gathering.

But there was no doubt during the bitter campaign that Proposition 13's opposition picked up on the same fear technique. Television and radio spots appeared in which police and fire fighters warned of dire losses of property and personal protection if the Jarvis Initiative won. The initiative's $7 billion reduction in property taxes, they claimed, would lead to fire and police budgets "dangerously curtailed"; "less (school) security"; and few emergency and paramedic units to serve local communities.

The two political consulting firms that were employed in the campaign were Winner/Wagner & Associates of Los Angeles, which worked for the Proposition 8 forces, and Butcher-Forde, a six-year-old firm based in Newport Beach which worked for the Proposition 13 supporters. While Winner/Wagner spoke freely about its techniques, Butcher-Forde remained closed-mouthed throughout the campaign.

Groups Opposing 13

Each campaign (Proposition 8 and Proposition 13) raised more than $1 million in private donations that were used primarily for TV and radio commercials. Although the Secretary of State's office was not scheduled to release final audited figures until late summer 1978, teacher groups opposing Proposition 13 appeared to contribute the biggest bloc of funds.

Teachers Against of Burlingame, near San Francisco, for example, contributed $114,763, according to required records on file with the Secretary of State. Burlingame is the headquarters for the California Teachers Association which, with 186,000 members, is the state's biggest teachers group and an influential force in shaping legislation in Sacramento. Other public employee groups, such as the California Fire Services Coalition which contributed $47,910, also turned in big chunks of anti-Proposition 13 campaign cash.

Other members of the coalition calling itself the "No on 13" committee included American Federation of State, County & Municipal Employees, AFL-CIO; Association of California Community College Administrators; California Community Colleges; California Democratic Council; California Federation of Labor AFL-CIO; California Federation of Teachers; California School Boards Association; California School Employees Association; California State Employees Association; California State Firemen's Association; California State PTA; Common Cause; Federated Fire Fighters of California; California Confederation of the Arts; California Democratic Party; and the Sierra Club.

In addition, several of the nation's largest brokerage houses contributed to the "no" campaign primarily fueled by fears that Proposition 13 would drop the rating on municipal bonds because there wouldn't be enough cash left over to pay the interest due on them. On top of this formidable lineup, many of California's biggest companies, led by outspoken Bank of America, the nation's largest commercial bank, led the assault on Proposition 13.

Meanwhile, the Jarvis forces used massive direct mailings orchestrated by the Butcher-Forde firm to raise their cash.

Butcher-Forde was able to put Milton Friedman, the Nobel Prize-winning economist, on TV with a message declaring that the measure was good government, while the Proposition 8 forces led by Winner/Wagner recruited nationally known economist Walter Heller to speak in opposition to the Jarvis Initiative.

The Jarvis Style

Neither side employed any politicians in radio and TV commercials. One of Jarvis' favorite tactics was to hit hard at the lawmakers in Sacramento. "The general public doesn't believe a damn word of what any politician says," Jarvis told Town Hall, a Los Angeles group of primarily business people. In fact, said Jarvis in an interview, he eschews all political support because of the strong undercurrent he feels exists of public distrust of politicians.

One of Jarvis' favorite political targets was Assembly Speaker Leo McCarthy, a San Francisco Democrat, with whom Jarvis debated Proposition 13 several times before live audiences and on television. In numerous speeches, Jarvis claimed the state has an ironclad constitutional obligation to fund the school system if Proposition 13 is approved. McCarthy said that was a blatant lie.

As it turns out, however, the governor and lawmakers then told the public that in the wake of the passage of the Jarvis Initiative, every dime that could be squeezed from the state's current surplus would go to schools, with the balance for county and local help.

Jarvis' oratorical style did turn off many listeners. "He has a kind of know-it-all attitude," said a member of a Los Angeles area school board after hearing Jarvis speak. "He's too aggressive in getting his points across."

But opponents made a serious mistake if they underestimated the Jarvis appeal. It appeared that Jarvis headed a rag-tag organization. He carried few notes in an old briefcase. He had the habit of making last-minute connections for transportation to engagements and, indeed, didn't even show up for some. And, he claimed, there were times when he forgot what group he was addressing until just minutes before he spoke.

Nevertheless since retiring in 1962 Jarvis had been study-
ing and speaking on tax issues to the exclusion of practically
everything else. His Los Angeles-based United Organization
of Taxpayers had been the vehicle for his crusade against
cutting taxes since that time. He had as firm a grasp of tax
issues as most Sacramento lawmakers and had debated these
issues for so long that he didn't need notes, much less
prepared texts.

"He's not a debater, he's a theatrical personality," said
Loran C. Vanderlip, a retired Sacramento lobbyist after
debating Jarvis before a mortgage bankers group in Palm
Springs. "Jarvis is entertaining," said Vanderlip. "I am not
entertaining. But I think the audience can cut through his
rhetoric."

Howard Miller, president of the Los Angeles City Board
of Education and a lawyer, agrees. Miller, who debated Jarvis
about a dozen times on the initiative and the merits of
Proposition 8, says you had to stick to the issues. "I try not
to get caught in emotion," said Miller. "I try to get onto the
facts. When Jarvis talked about fear, I talked about the shift
in taxes (under Proposition 13) from property to (higher)
sales and income taxes."

Miller said that one had to accept at the beginning of any
debate that Jarvis has "surface appeal." But, he said, "If you
keep talking about the facts it will catch up with him at
which point he starts his personal attacks."

Jarvis didn't show up at some of his scheduled meetings
with Miller who was Jarvis' most formidable debater.
Asserted Jarvis: "Miller is a nitpicker. I've had him up to
here."

On specific Proposition 13 issues, Jarvis was quick on his
feet. He claimed that the state really collects more than $40
billion in all taxes and fees, so losing about $7 billion won't
hurt much. Opponents have contended, however, that $26
billion is the true figure for state and local tax receipts. (U.S.

Census Bureau figures show in 1975-76 total revenue for the State of California and local governments was $31.8 billion, a figure that includes federal aid. Since the total had been growing by at least 10% a year, $40 billion was a reasonable estimate for 1977-78, even though firm figures were not available.)

As for the assertion that local school, fire, police and other special districts would be thrown into financial chaos by passing Proposition 13, Jarvis said, poppycock. Sacramento will take care of any local crises out of the big state budget surplus.

Jarvis was also asked why business was included in the initiative since it would get more than 60% of the tax benefits. Business would pay the same proportion of taxes, compared to residential property, under Proposition 13 as before, argued Jarvis. He added that it would be "unconstitutional to do it differently."

Jarvis also denied he was a puppet of the Apartment Association of Los Angeles County from which he draws a salary of $1700 a month, or that he stood to gain personally through passage of the initiative because he owns substantial amounts of property. Jarvis said that was completely wrong, that he owned no property in California except for his Los Angeles home.

PROGRESS OF THE CAMPAIGN

The strong antitax mood and Jarvis' organizational experience enabled him in a matter of weeks to collect 1.2 million signatures (nearly three times the required total) to qualify for the June ballot. This was a clear sign that from the start, Proposition 13 was going to be tough to beat as voter sentiment for lower property taxes began to snowball.

By the end of April, Jarvis told a *Los Angeles Times* reporter he felt he had the election won "hands down" without the TV and radio blitz that was used by both sides in May and the first week in June.

Two events in May gave Jarvis more momentum than even he had bargained for. Under pressure from the Los Angeles County Board of Supervisors, which had taken note of rocketing property reassessments, Los Angeles County Assessor Alexander Pope for the first time made public residential reassessment notices in advance of their actual mailing to homeowners. The information was informally disseminated in May to homeowners who dropped into their local assessor's office. In past years, this data wouldn't have been mailed to property owners until July.

About a third of the county's homeowners were reassessed in 1978 and the news they got wasn't good. Many found they had been reassessed 100% or more which meant they faced dangerously high tax bills unless Proposition 8 or 13 were approved. The news set up howls of indignation throughout Los Angeles County which already housed hundreds of thousands of key Jarvis votes. The news media picked up heavily on the sharply higher 1978 assessments and one could almost hear the swing in voter sentiment behind Jarvis at a time when the contest between 8 and 13 was almost even.

Apparently Pope was so shaken up by the tumult over the higher assessments that he suddenly instituted an assessment freeze for 1978 — in other words, no reassessments for that year — until lawmakers could come up with property tax reform.

This action triggered another howl from homeowners in Los Angeles County who were reassessed in 1976 and 1977, years when home values had begun to reach for the sky, prodded by mounting inflation pressures.

Proposition 8 backers argued that Pope's first action in releasing the reassessment information early dramatically raised the emotional level of the campaign, while subsequently freezing assessments made voters lose confidence in the credibility of government.

By the end of May the writing was on the wall. Public support for Proposition 13 had dramatically increased as the end of the month approached; a *Los Angeles Times* poll released May 28 found support for Proposition 13 had increased from 37% yes, 27% no in mid-March to 48% yes, 40% no in late May, with the balance undecided.

"The obvious conclusion is that the anti-Jarvis campaign has been ineffective and that homeowners — perhaps spurred on by recent property tax reassessments — have become more determined than ever to 'send government a message' in the form of a yes vote on Proposition 13," said *The Times*.

"Even among the 47% of those polled who felt Proposition 13 would reduce local government services, almost half said they would vote for the measure anyway," the newspaper said.

The Times poll also found general ambivalence and continued confusion over Proposition 8 with 35% of the respondents not favoring the measure, 34% backing it and 31% undecided.

Interestingly, the poll showed that union members had increased their support for Proposition 13, backing it 59% to 35% with 6% undecided although major union support had surfaced for Proposition 8 in terms of campaign contributions, according to the Secretary of State's records.

Blacks were overwhelmingly against the Jarvis Initiative, according to the poll — 68% to 22% with 10% undecided. Many members of minority groups rent apartments rather than own homes and the poll suggested they saw no advantages for them in Proposition 13 while the threatened reduction in county and city services would tend to hurt them more than more affluent homeowners. Also, since blacks lack seniority, they would tend to be the first employees dismissed in any wave of layoffs.

AFTER THE VOTE

Election night, June 6, saw a smashing victory for Proposition 13. And almost immediately every city, county and school district ordered emergency budget cutbacks while opening a legal assault on the amendment that took effect July 1, 1978.

Shortly after the election, several petitions challenging the constitutionality of Proposition 13 were filed with the state Supreme Court in San Francisco. Among the plaintiffs were the California Teachers Association, the California Federation of Teachers, the State Council of Service Employees Union, AFL-CIO, several big school districts, school officials, community colleges and several counties.

The suits claimed Proposition 13 revises the state constitution when it can, by law, only be amended; and that it violates the equal protection and due process clauses of the U.S. Constitution.

The state high court was expected to rule swiftly on the challenges so that no clouds hung over Proposition 13 as the state, counties, cities and other localities began their new financial year on July 1, the effective date of the Jarvis Initiative.

Meanwhile, the attention immediately shifted to three arenas. One was Sacramento, where Gov. Brown (see the Brown speech in Chapter 7) proposed using $4 billion of the state's surplus in direct aid and another $1 billion for loans to localities.

Wilson Riles, California's superintendent of public instruction, requested that $2.2 billion of that amount be used for aid to local school districts (see Riles statement, Chapter 7), which would still mean an effective cut of 6% to 10% in school spending, though more for some districts. (The legislature voted $2.0 billion on June 23, 1978.)

The second arena was California's localities and school systems. These jurisdictions had the responsibility for making thousands of immediate decisions about how to live within their suddenly reduced means. "No matter what we do," said assembly speaker Leo McCarthy, "I anticipate that at least 75,000 local government employees will lose their jobs in the coming months." Chapter 3 spells out the painful choices faced by the school boards and superintendents on the firing line.

The third arena was the rest of the nation. Passage of Proposition 13 gave impetus to a similar initiative in Oregon, as well as to tax limitation bills or amendments in Utah, Michigan, Washington State and elsewhere. A nationwide taxpayers' revolt, once dismissed as the pipe dream of a few malcontents, was suddenly a possibility.

"The silent majority found its voice and sent government and the bureaucracy a message loud and clear," said Charles Crawford of the National Taxpayers Union in Washington, D.C. "California is the two-by-four which has been used to get the mule's attention."

The real extent of the taxpayer revolt is yet to be determined; Chapter 4 will describe the status of tax limitation proposals and of public support for education around the country. There's no denying, however, the weight of the blow that fell in California on June 6. Both the lessons of the campaign there, and its aftermath for education and public services, will be remembered for many years to come.

3
On the Firing Line

"Devastating" . . . "Unbelievable" . . . "Catastrophic" . . . "Inhumane" . . . "Inconsiderate" . . . "A great suffering in morale" . . . "Poor public policy." These were the words used by California school administrators, teachers, union officials, curriculum coordinators and school board members in mid-June 1978 to describe how they felt about the passage of Proposition 13 on June 6, 1978.

To get reaction to the passage of the Jarvis Initiative, 20 school districts throughout California were surveyed within 10 days of the June 6 vote. An effort was made to contact districts throughout the state, so that different geographic areas and counties would be represented. In all, districts contacted are in 15 counties. In addition, an attempt was made to survey districts with diverse student populations. Thus, districts contacted range from the mammoth Los Angeles City School District, which has 722,000 elementary, secondary and adult education students, to the tiny Mariposa County School District, with fewer than 2000 pupils.

Similarly, an effort was made to contact districts with budgets and per pupil expenditures of varying sizes. The budget range for districts surveyed goes from a high of $1.4 billion for the Los Angeles City School District to a low of

33

$3.5 million for Mariposa County.

Per pupil spending for the districts surveyed ranges from a low of $1200 in Northern California's Marysville School District to a high of $2600 per pupil in Beverly Hills. By choosing diverse districts, the effect of Proposition 13 on districts of varying wealth could best be determined.

EFFECT ON DISTRICTS

In general, wealthier districts reeled hardest from the impact of the Proposition 13 vote, standing to lose 60% or more of their budget unless other funds were forthcoming. This is because higher spending districts derive most of their budgets from local tax revenues, whereas poorer districts have a higher proportion of state aid.

Proposals to use the huge state surplus for the aid to localities and school districts followed immediately after the vote on Proposition 13. Gov. Brown spoke to the legislature on June 8, proposing that the state use $4 billion of the surplus in direct grants, and a further $1 billion in loans. Wilson Riles, the state superintendent of instruction, recommended that $2.2 billion of this sum be earmarked for the public schools. The effect of such an appropriation would be a cut of between 5% and 10% in statewide spending on public education. Of the roughly $8 billion from the general fund that California districts spent on their schools in 1977-78, an estimated $4.5 billion to $5.0 billion came from local property taxes. Thus the loss from Proposition 13 would come to about $2.7 billion to $3.0 billion. Giving back $2.2 billion of this sum from the state would mean a net loss to local districts of $500 million to $800 million, or between 6% and 10% of total current spending. (Total school revenues in California, including building funds, cafeteria funds, special reserves, child development money, etc. were estimated at $10 billion before Proposition 13 and $9 billion as a result of the vote.)

TABLE 3-1
SCHOOL BUDGETS IN CALIFORNIA
BEFORE AND AFTER PROPOSITION 13

District	County	No. of Pupils	1977-78 Per Pupil Expenditure	1977-1978 Budget (in millions)	Anticipated 1978-79 Budget as a result of Proposition 13 (in millions)
Beverly Hills	Los Angeles	5,700	2600	$ 17.5	$10.5*
Ceres Unified	Stanislaus	4,500	1350	8.0	5.9*
Eureka	Humboldt	7,500	1200 El 1600 Hi	12.0	5.3*
Fresno	Fresno	54,000^A	1400	100.0	75.0
Irvine	Orange	12,000	1900	26.0	24.2**[1]
Los Angeles	Los Angeles	722,000^A	1675	1,400.0	648.0*
Mariposa County	Mariposa	1,720	1500	3.5	N/A
Marysville	Yuba	8,500	1200	16.0	10.6*
Palm Springs	Riverside	8,088	1600	13.0	4.3*
Palo Alto	Santa Clara	12,000	2400	31.0	15.9**
Pasadena	Los Angeles	24,500	1900	50.0	31.0* 45.0**
Pomona	Los Angeles	20,031	1260	37.0	25.9*
Rim of the World	San Bernardino	4,000	1630	10.0	5.0
San Diego	San Diego	119,897	1561	228.0	157.0
San Francisco	San Francisco	63,000	1991	194.0	92.0
San Luis Coastal	San Luis Obispo	7,270	1880	13.0	5.2
San Jose	Santa Clara	37,051	1507	70.0	36.0
Santa Clara	Santa Clara	20,000	1325	33.0	25.0-29.5** 16.0*
Stockton	San Joaquin	25,610^A	1692	57.7	44.7
Vallejo City	Solano	15,000	1300	23.0	18.0

A   Includes adults
*   Assumes *no* replacement of funds by state.
**   Assumes *some* replacement of funds by state.
1   Assumes $4.8 million loss on $29.0 million budget proposed for 1978-79.

The big unknown in this equation, however, was whether the state would replace the same percentage of dollars lost for each district in the state. The argument against doing so was one of equity: if the state is putting up most of the money, why should it permit Palo Alto and Beverly Hills to spend one and a half or two times per pupil what Marysville or Vallejo spend. Riles' recommendation was to hold the maximum cut for any district to 15% of its previous budget.

On June 23, the legislature approved a bill giving total aid of $5.0 billion to localities and schools, $4.1 billion in grants and $900 million in loans. Schools and community colleges were to get $2.267 billion; schools alone, $2.019 billion. Losses per district would range from 9% to 15%. Table 3-1 shows the impact of Proposition 13 *before* the infusion of this state aid.

As an example of the impact of Proposition 13 on wealthier districts, consider Beverly Hills. This district, which had a $17.5 million budget in 1977-78 and was spending $2600 per pupil, was looking at a budget cut of 60%, R. Cordova, in charge of business and purchasing, said. Palm Springs, with just over 8000 students and a $13.0 million 1977-78 budget, stood to lose $8.7 million and, with no legislative assistance, be left with $4.3 million in funds for the 1978-79 school year, according to Andrew J. Viscovich, superintendent.

Districts with less wealth stood to fare better, although the effect of Proposition 13 was still serious. Fresno, for example, was facing a 25% cut in its $100 million budget, bringing it down to $75 million. In normal times such a reduction would be devastating; compared to losses of 50% or 60%, however, it is more manageable.

In general, interviews with school districts throughout the state revealed that the loss in property tax revenues for their budgets ranged from between 25% to 68%. Few districts were found to have actual contingency plans; most had anticipated cuts and were ready to take action, pending decisions made by the California State Legislature.

While the closing of summer schools on almost a state-wide basis grabbed national headlines in the days immediately following the passage of Proposition 13, many districts were holding back on sending termination notices to district personnel, until they saw the magnitude of state aid. State law requires notice by March 15 before laying off "certified" or teaching personnel for the following school year. Some districts, such as the Los Angeles City School District, had covered themselves from the anticipated deleterious effects of passage of a property tax reform by sending "possible" termination notices before the state deadline of May 15 for certified personnel. Los Angeles didn't tread lightly, sending the "possible" termination notices to some 21,000 teachers. Most other districts, however, preferred to wait things out, and thus were faced with finding staff to cut among the ranks of classified, or noncertified, personnel when Proposition 13 became a reality.

Most of the 20 school districts contacted said they would attempt to maintain education programs at all costs. Peter Hagen, head of testing, research and development for the Pasadena Unified School District, said Pasadena would cut bricks and mortar first, personnel second and education programs last of all. Although districts were skeptical about how their educational goals would be achieved, they did appear willing to make a variety of sacrifices – pay cuts, suspension of merit increases, freezes on purchases – to maintain a semblance of educational order.

Steps being taken to effect budget savings in the wake of Proposition 13 passage can be divided into five general categories. These can roughly be classified as rearrangement of school personnel, involving termination and/or reassignments of existing staff; termination of summer school programs; termination of adult education programs; cutbacks in spending for materials, supplies and equipment; and changes in the traditional school day.

REARRANGEMENT OF SCHOOL PERSONNEL

Most districts moved slowly in terminating personnel, first because of uncertainty about what 1978-79 funding levels would be and second to maintain educational quality. (A third factor might be noted: if a district waited long enough, help, albeit temporary, might come in the form of state aid which would bail out a district from unpleasant "pink slip" decisions.)

As noted earlier, Los Angeles was one of the first districts to put "pink slips" in the mail; even in this case, the notices were of "possible" rather than definite terminations.

But since most school districts are heavily weighted by personnel costs — districts surveyed reported from 80% to over 90% of their budgets given over to this category — schools were forced, in the aftermath of the June 6 vote, to make belated plans for terminations. Because of a state law requiring notice to certified (teaching) personnel by March 15 of plans for termination in the next school year, classified (non-teaching) personnel were bearing the brunt of the cutbacks after passage of Proposition 13.

Among the districts proceeding with terminations as of mid-June was the 120,000-student San Diego School District. Unless it received offsetting state funds, Charles Glenn, assistant superintendent, said San Diego would fire 3444 school staff members, including 1900 teachers. These cuts would mean lopping off a third of the staff of 10,033.

Rudy Gati, superintendent in Santa Clara, a 20,000-student unified district, reported that district was "readying" pink slips in mid-June. Santa Clara said it had two options in the personnel area, neither attractive: cutbacks in classified staff and reductions in salaries.

Pomona, with just over 20,000 students, and Eureka, an upstate California district with 7500 pupils, had not sent "pink slips" by the March 15 deadline; both said most cutbacks would be made in non-teaching and temporary personnel.

Beverly Hills, one of the wealthiest California districts, gave 45% of its classified employees (85 in number) 30 days notice in mid-June; the Beverly Hills School Board also proposed a 10% pay cut for all remaining employees. Rim of the World, a high wealth district with a $10.0 million 1977-78 budget which was in danger of being slashed in half to $5.0 million, laid off 119 classified personnel and cut salaries 20% for remaining district employees. Palm Springs, another wealthy district, said it would lose 250 support personnel and not fill 40 teacher vacancies if state aid were not forthcoming.

Bright spots were few and far between, although some districts reported different plans to cope with Proposition 13. The Irvine Unified School District, which has a growing enrollment (up from 7000 in 1973-74 to a projected 13,000 for 1978-79), expected to be able to avoid cutbacks in staff provided it did not lose more than 20% of its proposed $29.0 million 1978-79 budget. Gene Hartline, head of business and purchasing, said Irvine was hoping to be able to absorb the loss in revenues through attrition and unfilled positions, claiming the "last to go would be teachers and materials." An Irvine school official was able to say that "If we were located 30 miles to the West, we would be in an area of declining enrollment, and be much harder hit than we are." (Nevertheless, Irvine, like other harder-pressed districts, intended to cut back severely on support personnel such as clerical and custodial workers.)

Elsewhere, Fresno took an innovative step and sent notices of possible demotions to administrative personnel. The district planned to replace teachers who retired or resigned with administrators. Even with these precautions and an admitted surplus "in the pot," Fresno admitted it faced the possibility of classified level job cuts and some administrative level terminations. Elsewhere, curriculum directors were preparing to step down to the principal level.

In other districts which did not immediately terminate staff to ease the bite of Proposition 13, belt-tightening measures were imposed. These included eliminating all over-time pay, putting an end to all extra-duty jobs (such as coaching football or acting as a department head), putting a freeze on hiring, failing to hire substitutes for maintenance and clerical personnel on vacation, ending the merit increase policy and rescinding salaried sabbatical leaves (San Luis Coastal figured it could save $40,000 simply by rescinding two salaried sabbatical leaves). Other districts moved to virtually shut down summer staff operations, thereby achiev-ing budget savings through enforced, "unpaid" vacations.

Overall, these steps were seen merely as stopgap measures whereby districts that had not yet made staff cuts postponed the almost inevitable termination of employees. Beleaguered California districts had still another problem in figuring out how to deal with the provisions of multi-year teacher con-tracts. Palo Alto noted that its three-year teachers' contract included a clause which allowed the school board to take emergency action to re-open the contract under certain conditions; the Proposition 13 crisis was considered an acceptable "condition." The district saw its options as honor-ing the current contract (difficult to do with a budget which might be slashed 53%), freezing built-in escalators in the contract or cutting teachers pay.

TERMINATION OF SUMMER SCHOOL PROGRAMS

In general, the first program to go in California following the passage of Proposition 13 was summer school, which was due to open in many areas just after the June 6 vote. One estimate of the cumulative effect of summer school closings in California was an economic loss of $150.0 million. The end of summer school will have the most deleterious effect in Los Angeles, where 7300 teachers will have no summer jobs and 371,000 kids will be out on the streets during the long, hot summer months. There has been a summer school program in Los Angeles every year since the Depression. It should also be noted that in addition to the elimination of summer school programs, other youth services, including recreation and park programs, may also be victims of Proposition 13, thus leaving hundreds of thousands of young Californians without organized summer activities.

Even as districts were terminating their summer school plans, some imaginative solutions emerged. One was in San Diego, where plans were formulated to allow high school students to take summer courses in community colleges. Another was in Palo Alto, where David Lake, president of Fearon-Pitman, a publisher of elementary and high school and special education materials, was working on plans to set up that district's planned-but-cancelled summer school program as a non-profit corporation. This would involve asking those who could pay to contribute, and attempting to raise scholarships for those who could not come up with the fee. Elsewhere, Los Gatos was putting its summer school program on a fee basis, Fresno was planning to offer a summer program for 265 students who needed credits to graduate and Irvine was formulating plans to provide summer courses for seniors needing just a credit or two to graduate.

TERMINATION OF ADULT EDUCATION PROGRAMS

Because of substantial in-migration from Mexico and the Orient, California has a variety of adult education programs which are incorporated into local school districts. In Los Angeles, for example, the 722,000-student population includes 138,000 adult students; the 25,000-plus Stockton City School District has an adult enrollment of 700. The fate of many of these programs was clouded by the passage of Proposition 13. As a temporary step, some districts suspended operation of their adult education programs for the summer months, pending determination of exact budget allotments for the 1978-79 school year. Among the districts to do this were the Los Angeles City School District, the Marysville Joint Unified School District, with 8500 pupils, and the Palm Springs School District with 8088 students. Reading between the lines of these steps, it is fair to assume that the programs won't easily be reactivated without help from the state or federal government.

CUTBACKS IN PURCHASES OF
SUPPLIES AND EQUIPMENT

Although many districts could not estimate how much their spending for materials, supplies and equipment would be cut back as a result of Proposition 13, those who did offer numbers projected cuts ranging from 50% to 100%. Many moved immediately to put a freeze on such purchases once Proposition 13 passed.*

San Diego said it projected *no* spending on materials because of the massive $71 million cut in its $228 million budget it might have to take as a result of Proposition 13. San Jose predicted a 20% decline in spending but said its cutbacks in materials would probably be greater than in other areas. Beverly Hills said its 1977-78 materials budget of $350,000 would drop to $180,000 in 1978-79 while Rim of the World anticipated a 50% cut in materials spending. Los Angeles, which spent $83.7 million on supplies, books and equipment in 1977-78, said it could not even estimate what this figure would be in 1978-79 and San Francisco, declining to estimate its spending in this area, nevertheless reported that materials spending would be the "easiest place to cut." Irvine, which spent $138,000 on textbooks in 1977-78 and $1.4 million on total textbooks, other books and supplies, admitted that figure would have to be reduced but did not

---

*The state itself gives districts $9.88 per elementary pupil for textbooks and materials annually, a sum not affected by Proposition 13.

know by how much. On the other hand, Pasadena, the district that said it would cut bricks and mortar first, people second and program last, predicted materials spending would hold steady. (Pasadena, where enrollment is declining, hopes to save $1.2 million by eliminating the junior high, or grades 7-8, portion of its four-level school system and integrating it with the K-6 level.)

CHANGES IN THE TRADITIONAL SCHOOL DAY

While it can be assumed that there will be some dramatic changes in the structure of the traditional school day and classrooms in California as a result of Proposition 13, districts surveyed the week following the June 6 vote could not provide definitive answers regarding the shape these changes would take. Few districts had actually prepared contingency plans; those which were planning staff cutbacks had generally not gone to the next step of figuring what effect on day-to-day operations the loss of staff would have.

Where definitive answers were available, San Diego, one of the districts with a contingency plan, said a shorter school day as well as the closing of small elementary schools would result from approval of Proposition 13. Los Angeles reported it was moving toward half-day scheduling; other districts, such as Eureka, also mentioned the possibility of split sessions. Obviously, cutbacks in staff will necessitate larger class size, though most districts hedged on how much larger. One district, Eureka, said increasing class size was not a viable solution because of state-imposed guidelines. California tries to discourage large classes by penalizing districts which exceed state-prescribed limits of 33 for kindergarten, less in grades 1, 2 and 3.

Most districts insisted that they would take all possible steps to maintain educational quality, and would make cuts in program, increase class size, shorten school hours, etc. only as a last resort.

LOS ANGELES: A CASE HISTORY

What happens to the largest school district in a state where voters approve a proposition to reduce and limit property taxes to 1% of market value? The Los Angeles City School District, charged with educating 722,000 elementary, secondary and adult students and operating on a $1.4 billion budget in 1977-78, literally had the fiscal rug pulled out from under its myriad services as a result of the June 6 vote. Faced with a loss of 74% of its operating budget, Howard Miller, president of the Los Angeles Board of Education, described the district on June 16 as "totally dependent on the state legislature for its return of funds."

According to Bill Rivera, special assistant to the Los Angeles school superintendent, Los Angeles fiscal problems are compounded by the fact that it is a large, business-oriented area which gets little money from the state: 74% of school funding in 1977-78 came from property tax revenues. Assuming no replacement of funds from the state, Los Angeles stood to lose $752 million as a result of the passage of Proposition 13: Los Angeles City's *loss* would thus be higher than any other budget in a California district. Even assuming receipt of proceeds from the state's $5.7 billion surplus, Los Angeles said it would come up $250 to $300 million short.

The city school district began taking steps to prepare for the anticipated effects of Proposition 13 months before the initiative passed. All teachers hired from 1959 on got notices of possible pink slips by the March 15 deadline, with a total of 21,000 certified employees receiving such notices. The district cancelled summer school shortly after passage of Proposition 13, a move which put 7300 teachers out of summer work and an estimated 371,000 kids "out on the street." The district also decided to close down during July and August, keeping open only essential services, such as the 300-man security force, integration personnel and lawyers. In all, an estimated two-thirds of the district staff were given an unpaid "vacation," with one-third staying on to perform essential services. Los Angeles estimated that closing summer school and shuttering most school services during July and August would save $48.0 million.

Elsewhere in the district, there was a recommendation to eliminate all busing, except that involved with implementing integration. Extracurricular activities, such as athletics and band, were expected to be suspended, along with most optional courses, as schools moved toward half-day scheduling.

Los Angeles also worried about remaining in compliance with federal regulations which allow it to qualify for some $100 million in federal education funds. An official pointed out that districts receiving federal money must comply with various federal laws, such as the Civil Rights Act of 1976. Since many of the teachers who will be dismissed will be those hired most recently, Los Angeles stood to lose many black and Hispanic teachers.

OVERALL IMPACT OF PROPOSITION 13

The reaction which cropped up most often in interviews with California school personnel in the 10 days following the June 6 vote was a "wait and see" attitude. Faced with the virtual certainty of staggering losses in their school budgets, most districts insisted they could not speak definitively about what would happen in the 1978-79 school year until word came down from Sacramento regarding what help the California State Legislature would provide. For this reason, much of the information provided by school districts in mid-June was conditional, with districts still speaking about "anticipated" cutbacks and "possible" terminations rather than providing hard and fast information about how schools would fare in the coming school year. The one certainty in mid-June was the decimation of California summer school programs.

Most school district personnel spoke about steps they would have to take because of the passage of Proposition 13 in a relatively matter of fact way, calmly reciting comparative budget figures which indicated that barring substantial legislative help, school spending could in many cases be *cut in half* in the 1978-79 school year. Table 3-1 gives comparative figures for 1977-78 and 1978-79, in some cases reflecting alternate assumptions — with and without additional state funding.

While school districts seemed to count on the increased state assistance that was voted on June 23, there was uncertainty, even gloom about what future years would bring. If the state aid was to be a one-time stopgap measure, what was the long-term prospect for public education in California? Hank Springer, head of the Los Angeles Teachers Union, came down hard on this point, noting that "There is no source of relief that I can see." Springer said that even if the legislature voted to apportion some of its surplus funds among districts, this would "only last six to eight months, after which we would have to vote new taxes or close schools." Asked to sum up his reaction to the June 6 vote, Springer, recalling that "Public education is the cornerstone of democracy," contended that he simply could "not believe what is happening in California."

California school districts also wondered how they could comply with state requirements in the wake of Proposition 13, including the mandates to come up with a balanced budget, operate for 175 days each school year and keep all certified personnel on their payrolls unless notice was given by March 15 for the school year beginning that September. Most districts felt there would have to be some reworking of existing state requirements because of the ramifications of the Jarvis Initiative. Although this was not specifically mentioned, districts will also have to determine how to remain in compliance with federal regulations on ethnic and sex ratios in order to continue receiving federal funds.

Asked for their own feelings on how Proposition 13 would affect their operations, administrators were quick to admit they were groping in the dark in much of their planning. A call to one California district revealed that all school personnel who could speak about district plans were out at a meeting on how to cope with Proposition 13. In San Jose, Jerry Weltzin, head of public information, admitted that "Every day we learn a little bit more, but we still don't know a lot."

While the consensus was that there was a need for property tax relief in California, a corollary feeling was that the Jarvis Initiative was not the way to effect change. R.N. McManus, superintendent of schools in the economically depressed Eureka School District, spoke for many when he hoped that a new funding formula would result from current chaos. "Even if they give us relief," he said, referring to the legislature, "we are still dealing with a unique situation and there will have to be some other solution."

Charles Glenn, assistant superintendent in San Diego, noted that Jarvis-Gann reaction was directed toward "legislators and bureaucrats" but the major impact will be felt by schools. "This just wasn't the way to change the California tax structure," he concluded.

Elsewhere, school personnel looked at Proposition 13 as the last straw added to a heap of earlier school cuts. In Santa Clara, Rudy Gati, superintendent, said that his district, which relies heavily on the property tax for school funding, had cut $4.0 million from its budget since 1975. Now, because of Proposition 13, Santa Clara is faced with cuts of between $3.5 million and $8.0 million on its proposed $35.0 million 1978-79 budget if the legislature comes up with some funds, and a $19.0 million shortfall if no legislative help is received.

It seems clear that the worst is yet to come for California districts. Even with help from the legislature, massive budget cuts will still be required and it is questionable how efficiently schools can do their job. The situation will be even worse in the 1979-80 school year than it will be in 1978-79, as the full effect of teacher and program cutbacks, not all of which can be implemented in fall 1978, begin to be felt.

Although the emphasis was on the black side of the Proposition 13 vote, those connected with education in California did see some positive effects of the June 6 vote. In Pomona, a school administrator said the lower cost of housing produced by Proposition 13 would enable black families to move in and thus help integration. Another district admitted the impact of Proposition 13 would speed its plans to reorganize its four-level system of schools, a reorganization necessitated by lower enrollments as well as budget constraints. Few administrators would venture to cite other positive effects of the voters' decision, however.

MORE STATE CONTROL INEVITABLE

The safest prediction about the impact of California's fiscal crisis on education is that the state will assume a far weightier role in public school finance and policy. From providing about 40% of the local education budget in 1977-78, the state will leap to a two-thirds share in 1978-79. It is difficult to see this proportion then going back down by much. Since Proposition 13 handcuffs local school districts' ability to raise property taxes in the future, while making passage of replacement taxes difficult, the state will have to find some way of making permanent its one-shot infusion of funds.

A shift of this magnitude, with the state suddenly providing the lion's share of elementary and secondary education dollars, will probably bring about more equal per-pupil expenditures from one district to another. (This change by itself could have far-reaching and dimly forseen effects on local property values. If Beverly Hills can no longer spend twice as much to educate its kids as Vallejo City, what then happens to property values in Beverly Hills?) But just as significantly, increased state funding cannot help but mean increased state control — over curriculum, policy and perhaps hiring and firing. With the state paying most of the salaries for those working in the schools, it seems only a matter of time before the state finds itself directly embroiled in contract negotiations — and perhaps in attempting to set wages and conditions of employment — across the 1000 school districts in California.

What all this state involvement will do to the concept of local control over education and to the desire of taxpayers to make local government services more responsive to those who use and pay for them, is only one of the ironies of the Jarvis-Gann Initiative.

The impact of Proposition 13 can be likened to Gesell's theory in educational psychology which calls for the breaking up of old behavior patterns before newer and more mature ones can be adopted. At some point, new educational behavior will emerge from California's shell-shocked teachers and administrators. But a state which has been an innovator in implementing early childhood education programs and reforming intermediate and secondary education programs will probably have to take two steps backward before it can take the next step forward.

4
The Revolt Spreads:
Other States

Once Proposition 13 had passed in California, attention turned to other states around the country where tax limitation or tax cutting proposals were active. Some proposals seemed likely to be put on the November 1978 ballots in their states, while others were in the early stage of talking or signature gathering. Moreover, the relation of these campaigns to education spending is complex.

Some states where antitax rhetoric flourishes, like Texas, actually have quite low property tax rates and school systems that are in good shape financially. Other states that seem riper for tax limitation, such as Illinois, contain many districts already living with straitened school budgets. Neither strong support for local school budgets, nor the absence of such support, is necessarily related to broader tax cutting campaigns in a given state. The following chapter will survey the situation in states and in particular districts, but readers must bear in mind that every local situation is unique.

MAJOR STATE CAMPAIGNS

Two days after the Jarvis Initiative swept to victory in

California, a referendum or initiative was filed with the lieutenant governor's office in Utah. Petitions were well along in Oregon, Idaho and Michigan, all pointing toward the November 1978 ballot, and tax limitation measures had also surfaced in Arizona and New Mexico, both historically low-tax states.

Petitions were also making the rounds in Colorado, Nebraska, Nevada, New York and Washington. The press reported similar activity in South Dakota and Montana. In Maine, a tax limitation group was working on petition wording. Clearly, something was astir in the country and, while the Jarvis petition was not the causative yeast, at least it was the lightning rod attracting taxpayer discontent.

Other movements may have surfaced after this book went to press, as wildfire Jarvis sentiment spreads. Activity in each of the 50 states and the District of Columbia is summarized at the end of the chapter.

While nothing is surer than death and taxes, this review of states suggests that taxpayers everywhere are determined to do something about the latter. Some of the tax cutting proposals may be poorly conceived, but all are indicative of a deep seated public mood. Often, it is obvious that elected officials have either been unwilling or unable to respond to earlier warning signals, but even states which had taken prior steps toward tax reform are finding that voters want more.

Only a few states with long histories of tax limitations or economic conservatism seem immune to the current wave of discontent. And some of these states, such as Ohio and Indiana, are finding that their tax systems are causing varying degrees of dysfunction and require adjustment or reform to meet today's needs. Even in New Jersey, where property tax relief is recent, some tinkering is needed to adjust its cap system.

The Idaho Initiative

Some of the property tax relief remedies suggested in

other states are interesting variations on Proposition 13 in California. For example, the Idaho Initiative, consisting of a 1% limitation on property taxes, differs from Jarvis in requiring that all property be valued according to its actual use. If passed, this initiative would become part of the Idaho code rather than the constitution, and as such, it could be altered by the legislature at will. This issue was red hot in Idaho, since the entire state legislature, plus the governor, the state superintendent of schools, both Congressmen and a U.S. Senator were all up for reelection in 1978. By late June the initiative had already collected some 20,000 of the 27,000 signatures required by a July 7 deadline.

Roughly half the funds raised from the property tax in Idaho go to the school system which is funded some 60% by the state. Although the present state superintendent of education has spoken out against the initiative, no detailed analysis had yet been made of its effect on the schools.

Barney Parker, superintendent of the 23,000-student Boise school system, says Idaho is getting the ripple effect of what's happening in California and "we're very concerned." If the Idaho Initiative goes through, its effect would be devastating, according to Parker, especially since Idaho doesn't have a surplus like California to stave off the immediate effects.

"The sad part" about the initiative, says Parker, "is that the good things those people signing petitions think are going to come to them because of it aren't really going to happen. The real benefits of the initiative go to businesses. Our sales tax, which is at 3%, would probably have to go up to 5%. Our income tax, which is already high at 7.5%, would have to go higher." Like many other school administrators, Parker feels people are signing petitions "because of frustrations with the federal government. The sad part is that they want to take away from the lowest level of government. They can't get to that senator, so they whip the guy at the bottom."

As an independent charter district, Boise doesn't have to

go to the people to get an increase above 27 mills ($27 per $1000 of assessed value) unlike most districts in Idaho. Nevertheless, Boise is asking only a 6.4% hike for 1978-79 over its current $32 million budget, the lowest increase in years.

"We are trying to be good stewards. We think we read the public very well," says Parker, explaining that Boise's annual expenditure per pupil is $1340, which is right at the Idaho average.

The Oregon Trail

In Oregon, an initiative petition filed by Jim Whittenburg, executive director of the Lobby for Social Concerns and Demands, sought a 1.5% ceiling on the property tax as a percentage of market value. By mid-June it had attracted 18,000 of the 64,000 signatures needed to go on the November ballot, but the vote in California led to a pickup in activity.

The effect on schools in Oregon was a topic of prime concern among educators. According to former Portland school board chairman Robert Ridgley, the initiative would decrease the average property tax paid by homeowners by one-third, thus wreaking havoc on school budgets.

Some Oregon school districts like Beaverton — with 20,000 pupils — have lots of new property coming on the tax rolls, and with regular reassessments, the tax rate per $1000 has been stable or declining. Even so, the overall property tax rate is 2% of market value. Beaverton's board and administrators have worked hard at community support so that annual school tax levy elections can be won. The district's $40 million budget is slated to rise to $43 million in 1978-79; careful trimming of administrative overhead and the charging of fees for some special programs, like driver education, have kept the increases moderate. Even with a tradition of excellent local support for school programs, "We're beginning to

hear the rumblings" of discontent over taxes, said superintendent Boyd Applegarth.

Initiative 358 in Washington

A new wrinkle in the petition area occurred in Washington State in mid-1978 when a state court ruled that Initiative
358 can be published in the newspapers and readers can clip
the copy and send in signatures by mail. Number 358 is
sponsored by a King County tax assessor and would limit
state property tax increases to 6% a year, not counting any
taxes on new construction, which is now growing very
rapidly. Washington localities already operate under the same
6% limitation.

If 358 becomes effective, it is "going to hurt us" on the
state level, says Gov. Dixy Lee Ray's press secretary. The
state could lose $75 to $100 million in revenues for the
two-year budget, 1979 and 1980, according to Charles
Hodde, state director of revenues. While Ray has been closely
examining the petition language, she has not yet been cam-
paigning against it.

Hodde says growth in taxable property in Washington is
such that the state could get 20% additional tax income in
1978-1979, not 12% as first estimated. Initiative 358 would
limit the increase to a maximum of 9%, 6% from already
existing property and a maximum of 2% to 3% for new
property coming onto the tax rolls. Most property is taxed at
$9.15 per $1000 assessed value. The state now gets over 40%
of total property tax receipts, which are distributed to school
districts on an equalized basis.* Capping the state property
tax thus puts a ceiling on school revenues.

Another petition making the rounds in the state would
tie total state tax increases to increases in personal income.

---

*Equalization refers to the process by which states distribute aid to
education funds in order to equalize per-pupil spending in local
districts.

This is not as far along as Initiative 358 and may instead be submitted to the legislature. The Washington Legislature has already okayed a bill to put a lid on special levies for education sought by local districts. The levy lid will reduce income from special levies from $350 million to $150 million in three years; new state taxes will have to fill the gap.

The Colorado Mood

Notoriously anti-tax Colorado has refunded more than $100 million in taxes to localities over the past four years. In the public's present mood, this isn't enough. Two petitions were circulating in the state with the November ballot as goal, each needing some 65,000 signatures to qualify. The most likely to succeed, sponsored by former State Treasurer Palmer Burch, would peg any increases in taxes to increases in the Consumer Price Index (CPI) and prevent state matching funds. The other, dubbed the Robertson Amendment, would limit taxes on owner-occupied homes to either 2.5% of market value or 5% of family income, whichever is lower; it had less support.

State officials said they could live with 7% in annual increases in the short run, but felt that in the long run the CPI, based on goods, generally rises more slowly than the cost of services purchased by the state. Colorado pays for 60% of education costs and is obliged by its constitution to run at surplus.

Local districts would be affected by both petitions. Market values in Colorado are skyrocketing and school districts are conditioned to ask for only what they know will pass.

The 25,000-student district of Pueblo for example has never gone to the public to ask for more than the percentage of fund increases allowed by the state. The intermediate step of additional fund approval by the state review board has always been sufficient. Pueblo's 1977-78 budget totalled some $44 million; 1978-79 will go up the same 10% already programmed by the state. According to Robert Freeman, superintendent, Pueblo is getting pressure from two sides. Pressures have come on the one hand from costly U.S. Department of Health, Education and Welfare requirements for such things as bilingual education and affirmative action as well as demands for new programs from the ethnically mixed community. On the other hand, pressures are coming from "the same machine you saw surface in California. We're going to hear more from them," says Freeman. "A lot of people are all dressed up and now have a place to go."

Freeman says that one of the things this group is against is bilingual education. "We always have too many administrators and too many frills. They are against physical education, bilingual education and so on. They can't vote a budget down because of the way the state works, but they can vote through a Proposition 13."

In 1977 the Colorado voters rejected a constitutional amendment called Amendment 10 that would have prohibited any increases in government spending except by a two-thirds vote of the electorate. "You couldn't get a two-thirds vote of the electorate if you had World War III," says Freeman. Although Amendment 10 lost substantially, the 1978 amendments were gathering momentum after California's vote.

Proposed Cap in Michigan

Another state where a move is underway to limit increases in government expenditures to the rate of increase of the CPI (unless the governor and two-thirds of both Houses agree) is Michigan. School support there still depends on votes at the local level. On June 12, 1978, 18 of 23 school district requests for additional funds were rejected.

The very carefully drawn Michigan proposal was the work of a group called Taxpayers Unlimited. It would also limit state-assessed valuation and keep the state from reducing its *proportion* of support for any local programs. For example, the state now supports the schools by some 45%, so it couldn't go below that. The proposal also says that the state shall not require any new programs or expand any programs without fully funding them.

The Michigan proposal had attracted 200,000 of 266,000 needed signatures by June 1978. If the proposal is voted in, raising new revenues for the schools would be a problem, according to Douglas J. Smith, special assistant to Gov. Milliken. Smith points out, however, that the CPI has been growing by about 6.5% annually and that it is questionable how much of this percentage would be needed in the face of the state's declining student enrollment. In the long run, increased personal income taxes could shift more support of the schools from the local level to the state.

Support for property tax limitations appeared to be snowballing despite enactment two years ago of Michigan's Rainy Day Fund Law. Effective in 1977, the law capped government expenditures, mandated a balanced budget and set up an economic stabilization fund for the state, whose economy is affected by the ups and downs of the auto industry. The law was intended to eliminate the need for across-the-board cuts as made by the state several years ago.

The requirement that Michigan school districts go to the voters for increases in tax levies to support education gives citizens ample opportunity to speak their mind on local budgets. In the four year period from 1974 to 1978, the City of Pontiac Public Schools won two increases in its tax levy totalling $6.75 per $1000, but its request for another $5.45 increase in 1978 went down to defeat, as did most such requests in Michigan districts. The 20,000-pupil district had wanted to boost its budget from $38 million to $40.3 million for 1978-79, but will now settle for a $1.3 million increase. "We've had to look hardest at personnel costs," said super-intendent Dana Whitmer, who expected the teaching staff of

1000 to drop by 60, mostly through attrition.

Tennessee's Amendment

During the furor over Proposition 13, much was made of the fact that Tennessee voters have already approved a constitutional amendment limiting state spending. Not a carefully conceived plan like the Michigan proposal, the Tennessee amendment consists of a brief and general statement limiting the rate of growth from state tax revenues to the rate of growth of the state's economy. Definitions of terms and mechanisms for implementation must be hammered out by a legislative committee which will make recommendations to the legislature in January 1979 for a law to make the amendment workable.

While the Tennessee restriction is not as drastic as those of Proposition 13, the acting superintendent of Chattanooga Schools, James D. McCullough, feels that the California vote created a general climate of accountability.

"It stimulated the reactions of the tax paying public," says McCullough. "Educators feel they are going to be watched more closely." School districts in Tennessee submit their budgets to another government body rather than to voters; the Chattanooga budget is approved by a city commission, for example.

SITUATION IN IOWA, WISCONSIN, MINNESOTA

The governments of Iowa, Wisconsin and Minnesota had been moving toward property tax limitations even before the California vote. Wisconsin recently cut some $200 million in property taxes, a 10% reduction, in addition to reductions in the past six or seven years that now total $1.6 billion annually. Much of that total of $1.6 billion has been returned to localities in the form of state aid to local schools. Wisconsin school districts are limited to maximum annual

9.5% increases in per pupil costs, but most have been holding increases under 7%. By the end of 1978, a special state commission on taxes was to have a report ready about what else can be done. Wisconsin's governor says that Proposition 13 shows that voters are "deadly serious" about reducing property taxes and that this ought to be heeded by every state.

In the state's largest school district, Milwaukee, Emmett Moll, acting head of the Division of Long Range Planning, says the Proposition 13 movement had "better be watched." Moll reports there is talk about replacing the property tax in Milwaukee with the sales tax, but that the city doesn't have much room to maneuver, not wanting to drive industry out with higher taxes.

So far, the district has been belt-tightening, not cutting; and is requesting a 5% hike for 1978-79 to $248.1 million, of which some $136.5 million will come from the property tax. The tax rate for schools is at $23.11 per $1000 of assessed value, with assessments at 85% of market value. Proposed cuts in athletics were restored in 1977 and the kindergarten program for 4-year-olds, which was thought to be in jeopardy, according to Moll, also seems secure now. However, in the face of declining enrollments (102,000 students now, down from 133,000 in 1970) the school board has been closing schools and reducing the number of teachers by attrition. Particular budget problems are caused by the new regulations regarding handicapped students, since the district requires additional teachers at higher salaries.

Iowa's Approach

In the last 10 years, Iowa has implemented a number of proposals generally moving school financing and some social services from a great reliance on the property tax — "obviously an unfair tax" according to one state official — to a much greater reliance on those taxes that the state collects, primarily the income tax. Sales taxes have been removed from foods and drugs.

Iowa was also the first state to start a state revenue sharing plan for local governments. The income tax has been made more progressive and some limits have been imposed on the rate of property tax assessments. On farmland, Iowa has gone to a different method of assessment so productivity is the basis, rather than market value. Assessments on urban homes can go up at no greater percentage than those on farmland.

In 1971, a state school foundation plan was adopted under which the state has put increasingly substantial sums of money into the schools. Basic foundation aid will account for a little over 80% of school costs in another five years, up from 77% now. Iowa also put some lids on the amounts of growth allowed in taxes by local governments and school districts.

Minnesota Reforms

Minnesota also has a long history of tax reform, but the state constitution does not have a referendum procedure. The 1967 Property Tax Relief Act enacted a sales tax and the state then funneled receipts of sales and income taxes back to school districts and local units as aid payments. Although the property tax paid about 70% of all local expenditures in Minnesota 10 or 12 years ago, it now supports only 30%. California's property taxes increased by 120% since 1966; Minnesota's, by contrast, have increased by 54%. The state ranks about eighth in the nation for the per capita burden of its income tax, though approximately 35th for its property tax.

Other Minnesota reform features are a circuit breaker* for

---

*A provision that property taxes cannot exceed a certain percentage of income.

individual taxpayers if the income tax is low enough and the property tax high enough. Even so, Minnesotans are still upset regarding the property tax because it is not based on ability to pay and is considered a regressive form of taxation, according to Dorothy McClung, research attorney for the Minnesota Department of Revenue. The state currently imposes a mandatory local effort of 27 mills ($27 per $1000) on assessed value in each school district, with the rest of the costs of education picked up by a state foundation aid formula based on per pupil units. Local units of government can only increase levies by 6% a year.

Not surprisingly, the deputy superintendent of St. Paul Schools, Kenneth Berg, has seen no signs of intensifying taxpayer discontent. Berg agrees there is a general concern regarding the costs of government, but says it doesn't focus on the schools. Because Minnesota sets a funding limit and because the school board doesn't have the power to raise that levy, only lower it, schools get less of a reaction from taxpayers. At St. Paul's last public hearing on the budget, only four citizens showed up.

In rural areas, however — and much of Minnesota is rural — Berg says that the school becomes more of a focal point for the community "and taxpayers see more of what they get for the money they spend. You lose that unity in an urban area where there are so many schools."

Ohio

No discussion of property tax limitations as they affect public schools would be complete without attention to the state of Ohio, traditionally a low tax state with one of the toughest property tax limits in the country. For almost 50 years, the Ohio constitution has limited the property tax that may be levied without a vote of the voters to 1% of the true market value. Ohio laws have made this constitutional man-date even tougher, since the rule of 10 mills ($10 per $1000) is based on assessed value, which is only 35% of market value. When property is reappraised and assessments are raised, the state also has to reduce the rate by law.

Public voters can override Ohio limits by voting millages. That's the principal way property taxes are actually levied in Ohio, according to Richard Levin, research director of the Ohio Department of Taxation, whereas elected officials establish property tax rates in California. The average property tax rate in Ohio is about 45 mills ($45 per $1000 on assessed value), or about $16 per $1000 of market value.

Since 1969, Ohio voters have been rejecting 60% of property tax hikes for schools. Some 100 of Ohio's 616 districts, including populous Cleveland (113,000 students) and Columbus (90,000 students), were in danger of running out of funds and having to close shortly after their September 1978 opening. Some districts were in danger of not opening at all. Obviously, this taxpayer revolt preceded Proposition 13, although the two were linked by the press. Roger Lulow, executive director for administration of the State Education Department, claims Ohio is now suffering the consequences of its property tax laws.

To keep schools open, Gov. Rhodes and legislative leaders were backing stopgap measures which consist of pumping an extra $56 million into the state's foundation formula and a $50 million loan fund for those not helped by this addition. A permanent solution to the state's education funding problems must come from a new foundation formula or reworking of the old one declared unconstitutional in December 1977. Yet legislative action on new school finance seemed unlikely until after the November 1978 elections.

The budget director for Columbus Schools, Ian Pottinger points out that the district's June levy loss was nothing new. It was the district's third defeat since 1976. Columbus had $118.2 million available for the calendar year 1978, though its need is estimated at $135.3 million. Unless the legislature acted, the district could run out of funds by mid-November.

It would then have to close schools, reopen in January 1979 and make up the lost days by June to fill out the 180 required by the state. The school system's operating tax rate is 26.31 mills ($26.31 per $1000); assessment is 35% of market value.

Pottinger sees little relationship of events in Columbus to those in California, since Ohio's tax level is about one third of the Golden State's. One explanation for Columbus — and Cleveland — vote failures, according to Pottinger and to Joseph L. Davis, Columbus superintendent, is that both districts are under desegregation orders which makes a lot of people unhappy. Both Davis and Pottinger agree further that there is general voter dissatisfaction over taxes. They stress that although Ohio's property tax is low, Ohioans hit by inflation don't look at what other states are doing, just at what they paid last year. (To people who encounter Ohio property taxes after coming from other states, on the other hand, Davis says "Ohio seems like heaven.")

Noting that proposals exist in the state legislature to shift much of education funding to the state income tax, Pottinger states most Ohio citizens are going to "sit back and defeat levies until the legislature decides to do something about it."

Whatever happens, Davis feels that Columbus already cut as much as possible: 730 people were dropped from the payroll in 1977 alone; eight school buildings were closed in September 1977, with 13 more to be shut in September 1978; and tuition charges were instituted for summer school. The textbook budget has been cut in half. "Where we were allocating $600,000 to textbooks, we have cut to $300,000," says Davis. "You can see that we are building up a backlog of needs."

Davis also mentioned that elementary school library programs had been reduced sharply through staff cuts. To prove that Columbus has already reached the bone, Davis cited the following statistics: of the eight Ohio big city districts, Columbus ranks last in cost per pupil ($1362); of the 14 large big city systems in the country, Columbus ranks 13th in cost per pupil (only Memphis is lower); and of 185 city school districts in Ohio, only three spend a lower percentage of their operating dollar on administration.

Proposition 13 has gotten an enormous amount of visibility everywhere, according to Davis, who basically believes that it will have relatively little impact on his low tax state. "On the other hand," Davis says, "it may well lead to some sort of a ceiling on our total tax program."

ILLINOIS AND NEW YORK

Proposition 13 has caused renewed efforts in the Illinois legislature to limit state and local taxes. A "Taxpayer Rights Amendment" sponsored by Republican Rep. Donald Totten would limit the growth of both property tax bills and state taxing powers. Even if passed by the legislature in the next session, the amendment could not reach the voters until 1980.

In the gubernatorial campaign between incumbent Gov. Thompson and Democratic candidate Michael Bakalis, taxes and state aid to education were emerging as issues. Bakalis argued that the state should assume a greater share of local education expenses.

For the state's largest district, Chicago, with 498,000 students, even the present level of 50% state support isn't enough. The district's budget of $1.2 billion is tightly controlled, and Chicago has had no increase in the property tax rate of $35.90 per $1000 of assessed value since 1971. Property is assessed at 33% of market value. Talk of an increase raised such a hue and cry at a board of education committee meeting that the subject was quickly dropped.

The present superintendent, Joseph P. Hannon, has put a tight rein on expenditures, paring the deficit to $50 million from $97 million in three years.

In suburban Evanston, voters are also keeping a tight rein on spending, having voted down a proposed $2.5 million increase by two to one.

New York

New York State ranks second only to Alaska in terms of total tax burden per capita, with high income taxes, a statewide sales tax and often astronomical local property taxes. Some relief on income tax was passed by the state legislature prior to 1978. Property tax reform would likely be spurred by the decision of a Supreme Court judge on June 23, 1978 that the present system using the property tax for school finance was unconstitutional. Appeals were certain.

Passage of Proposition 13 in California immediately made tax limitation an issue in New York's gubernatorial campaign. The Republican candidate, Perry Duryea, proposed a 20% reduction in state taxes and a local property tax freeze.

Like Chicago, the mammoth New York City school system with its 1 million students has been in precarious fiscal shape since 1975-76. In that year the district's operating budget was slashed $284 million to $2.25 billion and 20,000 full-time equivalent positions cut from its 119,800-member staff. Further cuts were made in succeeding years. The loss of more than 75,000 elementary and junior high pupils during roughly the same period offset some of the cuts, which nevertheless drastically curtailed services to remaining students. The elementary and junior high school day was reduced by two periods a week beginning in 1975-76 and high school electives were trimmed.

The city system may also be recovering health. The full school day was restored September 1977 and electives were restored. A new School Chancellor, Frank J. Macchiarola, took over from retiring Irving Anker July 1, 1978. The 1978-79 budget was expected to total about $2.85 billion; certain mandated and fixed costs such as pensions, over which the city has no control, go up every year.

Rochester, Buffalo and some 48 other New York State city school districts have faced their own budget crises as a result of a State Court of Appeals ruling enforcing constitutional limits on property tax collections. Emergency state grants and loans were passed in June 1978 to prevent cuts in those budgets.

School districts that are not in cities must go to the voters for budget approval in New York, and even wealthy suburban districts accustomed to community support have noted increasing difficulty in passing their budgets. Once again, the fact that the school budget is the only government expenditure that citizens can actually vote on is often a factor when a budget is defeated.

TEXAS AND ARIZONA

With most of the school districts in the nation experiencing shrinking enrollments, the fact that many school systems in the South and Southwest have been able to maintain enrollments or increase them slightly is evidence of a healthier environment for school finance.

A rising population means new property coming onto the tax rolls, so even with tax rates stable the budget can increase year by year. Moreover, property tax rates in this area are notoriously low. Arizona law limits annual school budget increases to 7% per pupil, unless the board goes to the voters for an override election. In the spring of 1978, even districts with a recent history of winning such elections found the going tougher. Six of seven Phoenix elementary districts lost budget votes, while the Tempe District No. 3, with 13,000 pupils had the same experience. The refusal of voters to approve an $839,000 addition to a $22 million budget means eliminating 17 teachers and a 3% salary increase.

Despite the already low property taxes in Arizona, the state is the scene of a campaign for a constitutional amendment that would limit future tax spending to increases in personal income.

Low Taxes in Texas

Texas, with a per capita tax burden well below the national average and no corporate or personal taxes, basks happily in the rosy affluence of growth and mounting oil and gas revenues. The state has been passing along significant increases in education dollars to districts every few years. Its urban school districts are in good shape, some of the smaller ones less so, and the trend is toward tax equalization.

Still, a feeling persists among Texans that taxes are too high. A cap on state spending failed by one vote in the last session of the legislature and may come up again. Taxation loomed as a major campaign issue in the state in summer and fall 1978.

Texas' largest districts are far healthier than other big cities in the U.S. With $1 billion worth of new property coming on the tax rolls annually, the stable 205,000-student Houston district hasn't changed tax rates or assessments in 18 years. Its 1978-79 budget is $267 million, an increase of $17 million from the previous year. Houston's tax rate is $9.00 for $1000 of assessed value, well below the state statutory limit. Property is assessed at 29% of market value.

At the Dallas Independent School District, Larry Ascough, associate superintendent for communications, thinks there is no doubt "that the California vote has set off tremors across the country" even though "in this part of the country we don't know what taxes are." Ascough cites the first city bond defeat in 30 years, occurring the Saturday after the California vote.

The Dallas tax rate is $14.20 per $1000, with assessment at 75% of market value. Its 1978-79 budget is tentatively set at $200.9 million, up $6.9 million. Enrollment is some 138,000 and declining since 1970. Dallas has been reducing teaching staff through attrition, but maintaining favorable pupil/teacher ratios of 24 to 1 in grades K-3 and 27 to 1 in grades 4-12. Dallas still has "a lot of optional programs for kids, compare to other big cities," says Ascough.

THE NATIONWIDE IMPACT

One of the obvious lessons of this survey of state and district budgets is that while taxpayers everywhere would like to pay less taxes, the situation in California remains somewhat unique. Few states have experienced as sharp an increase in local property values; some have already moved to ease the dependence of school financing on the property tax. Even in states like Michigan and Ohio, where local voters have rejected school tax levies, the impact of these votes was to hold budgets or tax rates constant, not to institute the magnitude of cuts seen in California.

"These things go in cycles," said a budget expert in Maine, referring to the wave of tax limitation proposals. "Right now people are feeling the crunch." The tug of war between people's demands for public services and taxpayers' resistance to paying for those services is a constant one, and no single year's battles will ever decide the issue.

The following state by state rundown summarizes the status of tax cutting movements and their implications for school finance as of summer 1978. Chapter 5 then considers the alternatives to the present tax structure, with its emphasis on property taxes, as a way of supporting the nation's schools.

State by State Summary
of Tax Measures, June 1978

Alabama
Lowest personal property taxes in U.S. didn't make this state immune to tax reforms. A recent court-ordered assessment at 100% market value to correct extreme and unfair disparities will mean massive increases especially beneficial to schools, since these are funded from property taxes. Special legislative session may cap increases.

Alaska

Nothing similar to Proposition 13 is active. Largest burden of taxes is borne by oil and gas companies. State assumes nearly 100% of the cost of basic education, while localities bear the cost of extras.

Arizona

Petitions similar to Jarvis were being circulated. A special legislative session in 1979 had been called pre-Jarvis to review whole state finance system. A state spending limitation of 7% of total personal income will be on the November 1978 ballot. Local school budgets for maintenance and operation can grow no more than 7% per child per year without voter approval.

Arkansas

No proposal had been made to lower property taxes, which are already among the lowest in the U.S.

California

Passed Proposition 13 limiting property taxes to 1% of market value on June 6, 1978. (See chapters 2, 3.)

Colorado

An antitax state which has refunded more than $100 million to localities in taxes the last four years. Two petitions were circulating; the most popular would limit tax increases to increases in the Consumer Price Index.

Connecticut

Nothing was hapening at the state level. Municipalities control property tax rates so changes would be made at local level.

Delaware

Although unrelated to Proposition 13, two tax measures were

in the works, a budget cap and a call for a greater majority to enact tax legislation. State has had problems in balancing its budgets for years.

District of Columbia
Anticipating taxpayer needs, District put in homeowners exemption and circuit breaker for elderly. The day after Proposition 13 passed, it increased the exemption, extended circuit breakers and split the property rate for first time so homeowners pay less. Schools have to make do.

Florida
Bill similar to Proposition 13 was introduced the day following California vote but on last day of legislative session. It may be reintroduced in 1979. Florida property taxes are low and limited. Although state has increased spending, many school districts are hurting. Florida pioneered the "Truth in Taxation" law which reassesses homes every year in the light of market value, then reduces the tax rate so no additional revenue is generated. The taxing unit also must hold well-publicized hearings twice to increase property taxes.

Georgia
Property taxes have increased dramatically. Although the Assembly rejected legislation limiting further increases, it established a Tax Reform Commission to recommend changes. State seems ripe for some kind of action.

Hawaii
Education is funded 100% by state. Property taxes are low; there is no initiative process in constitution.

Idaho
Petitions were being signed to make 1% property tax limit part of the Idaho code rather than the constitution. Education is funded about 60% by the state from property tax.

Illinois

Proposition 13 caused renewed efforts in legislature to limit state and local taxes; no proposals could reach the ballot until 1980. Property tax limitation would affect schools. Gubernatorial candidates square off regarding meaning of school budget defeats, Governor Thompson claiming these indicate voters want governments to hold the line, while candidate Bakalis (former State Supt. of Schools) says locals want state to provide a greater share of education expenses.

Indiana

Property tax reform in 1973 reversed percentages of state and local share of education to 70% state, 30% local. State school aid pegged to 1973 average daily attendance figures cramps growing suburban districts. Districts are not allowed to raise taxes. A Proposition 13 move seemed unlikely.

Iowa

Over past 10 years, school finance has been moved from heavy reliance on property tax to state taxes, primarily the income tax. Current state share of education costs is at 77% and increasing.

Kansas

Tax structure and its impact are currently under study; interest is high. Average statewide school support is 45%, with aid equalized.

Kentucky

State pays two thirds of local school budgets and property taxes can't be raised without voter approval. Average property tax is 1% of market value.

Louisiana

Nothing was to be introduced into legislature except perhaps a congratulatory message to California since deadline for legislation had passed. Property tax collections are among lowest in nation.

Maine
Tax limiting petition was being put together. All budgets are under careful scrutiny. "Robin Hood" statewide property tax to equalize school funding was repealed by referendum in December 1977.

Maryland
Significant property tax reform occurred prior to Proposition 13. Some petitions were reported circulating for further limits.

Massachusetts
Reaction to Proposition 13 caused a bill limiting property taxes to 2.5% to be filed late in the legislature. Ceiling would be high because of heavy reliance on the property tax. Also pending is a proposed amendment to limit state spending, through a complicated formula based on personal income.

Michigan
A 1977 Rainy Day Fund law moved toward a government expenditures cap. Strong support for a petition seemed likely to put a constitutional amendment before voters in November 1978 limiting revenue increases to rises in the Consumer Price Index. Local voters must approve increases in property tax levies for school support.

Minnesota
Property tax reform is recent; income tax reform is now the top issue. State school support has been increasing (over 50% now); there is mandatory local minimum of 27 mills on assessed value in school districts.

Mississippi
Education receives the lion's share of the state budget (60.1%). The state income tax increased 120% over past 10 years. Lots of talk and interest in Proposition 13 were reported as a result of general unhappiness over taxes.

Missouri
Governor hailed passage of Proposition 13, advocated limits on state spending and taxation.

Montana
Some Jarvis-Gann-type petitions were reported circulating. Property taxes were reduced $100 per owner-occupied home during the 1977 legislative session. Legislature doesn't meet again till 1979.

Nebraska
Broad-based petition drive was launched in spring 1978 to place 5% increase limitation on budgets of local taxing districts, including school districts. Earlier lid proposals by governor were rejected by legislature.

Nevada
Several plans to reform property tax were in the works but nothing will come to pass till the next session of the legislature. Petition was being circulated to base taxes on amount paid for home.

New Hampshire
New Hampshire is the only state in the nation without a statewide sales or income tax. The governor backed a tax-limiting bill introduced into last days of the legislature to require all state, county, municipal and school budgets to be balanced and contain a surplus of at least 1% annually. Local property tax increases could not exceed 5% without two thirds vote of voters in the locality.

New Jersey
Cap law was part of tax reform and income tax package when state refinanced schools under court order July 1978. School district caps have caused some problems and some adjustments may be legislated.

New Mexico
1977 ceiling of 10% was imposed on annual property tax increases. Property taxes are low. State pays high percentage (upwards of 80%) of school funding. Most of tax revenues come from income tax and severance taxes (gas and oil).

New York
Post Proposition 13 petition was circulating. Democratic Gov. Carey took credit for tax relief measures under his administration including small cuts in personal income tax, while Republican candidate Perry Duryea called for 20% reduction in taxes, local rate freeze and a constitutional amendment smacking of Proposition 13.

North Carolina
Bill introduced into legislature in hectic last days of session called for tax study commission to report to governor by Jan. 1, 1979.

North Dakota
A circuit breaker program has been suggested to legislative commission preparing for 1979 session, but circulating petitions concern income tax reductions. Schools are funded at 60% by the state from income and sales taxes.

Ohio
Some legislators said the time was ripe to introduce a bill limiting overall taxation; state has already among toughest property tax limit laws in the country. People vote on property tax millages and have been reluctant to raise extra

funds for schools; budget defeats in Columbus, Cleveland, et al are part of a long tradition. Reworking of a school finance law declared unconstitutional won't come till after November 1978 elections.

Oklahoma
No action similar to Proposition 13 was reported in this state where the income tax is the primary revenue source and property taxes are low.

Oregon
Petitions to limit property tax to 1.5% of market value were gathering momentum. Voters could decide in November 1978.

Pennsylvania
Since the state lacks the referendum/initiative procedure, property tax reform depends on the state legislature. A 1977 act authorizing increased school subsidy was intended to provide some property tax relief. School districts can also levy a local 1% wage tax.

Rhode Island
There is some sentiment for shifting education support away from the property tax, which is set locally. Increases can be no more than 8%.

South Carolina
Some tax action was anticipated in January 1979 when the next legislative session convenes.

South Dakota
The legislature does not meet again until January 1979. There were press reports of signatures being gathered to put a tax limitation measure on the 1980 ballot.

Tennessee
A constitutional referendum in March 1978 voted limits on state spending, but definitions and mechanics will be worked out by the legislature. Local school districts get budget approval from governmental units rather than voters.

Texas
Taxation was to be a major campaign topic in the fall 1978 elections. Even though property taxes are low compared to other states, there is still local resentment. Urban school districts are in pretty good shape, small to medium districts less so. The trend is toward tax equalization.

Utah
An initiative to limit property taxes to 1% of value was filed one day after Proposition 13 passed.

Vermont
No statewide tax limits were actively being supported. Residents pay property taxes locally; town meetings determine school budgets. Schools are still funded largely by property taxes; the state covers 20% of education costs.

Virginia
No proposals similar to Proposition 13 were pending. Virginia's constitution requires a balanced budget.

Washington
Two petitions circulating. One would limit revenues from state property tax increases to 9% annually, the other would tie state spending to personal income. Local tax levies for education are already limited to 6% increases annually.

West Virginia
No proposals were active. Annual property taxes averaged half the national total in 1976.

Wisconsin
The state has been cutting property taxes and increasing state aid to education. School districts limited by law to a 9.5% annual increase in per pupil costs.

Wyoming
No specific proposals were reported. Property taxes are a county issue.

5
The Alternatives to Drastic Cuts

In the aftermath of California voters' overwhelming approval of Proposition 13 on June 6, 1978, the drama of the taxpayer revolt has overshadowed the more difficult job of balancing needed public services against citizens' reluctance to keep on supporting the rising cost of government. Among the toughest problems to be faced is that of finding new ways of financing education in the U.S.

TEARING DOWN THE STRUCTURE

As in many revolutions, the emphasis in the early period of the so-called taxpayers revolt was on tearing down the existing structure, in this case the property tax system, without offering a viable alternative. This is exactly the situation which Californians faced following the Proposition 13 vote. By voting to limit property taxes to 1% of market value, they had thrown school districts throughout the state into financial chaos, pushed the County of Los Angeles to the brink of financial insolvency (the county government, without a bail-out, would have run out of cash on July 13, 1978) and paved the way for massive cuts in public services, including police and fire protection and sanitation collection.

Temporary state aid will mitigate the first year effects of this fiscal crisis, but in the long-run a new financial basis for public education and other local services is required.

As California legislators, school boards and administrators, local government officials and others struggled to make order out of the post-June 6 chaos, various alternatives to the drastic tax cut measure enacted in California became the subject of public debate. Some of these proposals were not new, but were catapulted into prominence because of intense interest in California's fight in particular and in the antitax movement in general.

Central to understanding what impact the approval of Proposition 13 will have on financing public education in California is an historical perspective on how public schools have traditionally been funded. The major portion of funding for public education has generally come from local governments, which in 1975-76 provided 47% of school funding. The next largest share was provided by state governments, 44%, and the smallest share came from the federal government, 9%. In recent years, as Table 5-1 shows, the states have played an increasingly larger role in education funding, with the local share declining somewhat and the federal share increasing slightly.

LIBERAL ALTERNATIVES:
NEA AND OTHER PROPOSALS

One clearly articulated alternative to drastic tax cuts such as Proposition 13 is the National Education Association (NEA) alternative, which says "a viable long-range solution to the financial crisis afflicting public schools (is) a system in

TABLE 5-1
PERCENT OF SCHOOL REVENUE DERIVED
FROM VARIOUS SOURCES

School Year	Federal Sources	State Sources	Local/Other Sources
1955-56	4.6%	39.5%	55.9%
1965-66	7.9	39.1	53.0
1966-67	7.9	39.1	53.0
1967-68	8.8	38.5	52.7
1968-69	7.4	40.0	52.6
1969-70	8.0	39.9	52.1
1970-71	7.2	40.0	52.8
1971-72	8.0	40.2	51.8
1972-73	7.9	40.6	51.5
1973-74	7.5	43.0	49.5
1974-75	7.8	43.6	48.6
1975-76	8.8	43.9	47.4

SOURCE: U.S. Dept. of Health, Education & Welfare, National Center for Education Statistics, *Digest of Education Statistics*, annual editions.

which broad-based, less regressive taxes such as the federal income tax provides a full one-third of the costs in our nation's schools." NEA suggests that schools be funded equally by federal, state and local sources, with each contributing one-third of the cost. The local property owner's burden would thus be lightened from as much as 80% of the total cost to 33%, which NEA calls "a fair share."

NEA, which blasts Proposition 13 as a "brutal and repressive measure," supported the introduction of legislation in Congress in 1978 called the Education Act of 1978, which called for an expanded federal commitment to the public schools and aid to state and individual taxpayers. The measure would also have established a national policy for assisting schools in financial stress, and provided what NEA called "a start toward reducing the burden on the property owner." The Education Act of 1978 was an early victim of Congressional deliberations on an extension of the Elementary and Secondary Education Act (ESEA); looking beyond the demise of that legislation, it seems unlikely that the federal government, facing a $50.0 billion budget deficit of its own, is going to increase its share of public school funding from 9% to 33%.

Underlying NEA's contention that the federal government should pay a dramatically larger share of the cost of education is the acknowledged fact that the federal government has greater taxing powers than either states or localities and is in the best position to distribute funds. This same view has been adopted by Michael Harrington, author of *Socialism* and *The Twilight of Capitalism* and also national chairman of the Democratic Socialist Organizing Committee. Harrington is an avowed "man of the democratic left" who confessed in a June 15, 1978 *New York Times* Op-Ed page article that he was "appalled" by the passage of Proposition 13 in California. Nevertheless, Harrington found a "core of progressive truth in the tax revolters' complaint." In Harrington's view, relief from what he calls "incredibly regressive" state and local taxes could best be achieved by abolishing "all the taxes in the United States except for a radically reformed federal income tax, which would actually distribute its burdens according to the ability to pay." Continuing, Harrington says that Washington, which he calls "not only potentially the most just, but already the most efficient collector of taxes, would give states and municipalities their share according to a computerized formula based on population as somewhat weighted to take account of social problems."

CONSERVATIVE EFFORTS AT TAX REFORM

The liberal proposals for tax reform are anathema to conservative groups and individuals, as represented by the California-based National Tax Limitation Committee and by economist and Republican adviser Arthur B. Laffer.

Interest in tax reform sparked by Proposition 13 and the nationwide visibility of Milton Friedman as a columnist for *Newsweek* have propelled the views of the NTLC, of which Friedman is a founder, into prominence. The committee's basic aim is to place ceilings on the spending powers of states by amending their constitutions; its goal, in effect, is to tie state spending increases to growth in personal income, something which was *not* done in California, where property tax increases were tied to rises in the assessed valuation of property. The committee, accordingly, sees "overall tax limitation as the power of the people to shape our society and our destiny." Its tenets were generously supported in the spring of 1978, when some 200 persons from 38 states attended, at their own expense, the NTLC convention in Illinois.

Another highly visible exponent of conservative tax reform is Laffer, whose Laffer Curve theory revolves around increasing the tax base by tax cuts. Laffer contends that tax rates have two effects on revenue: an arithmetic or accounting effect, which says that if you lower the tax rate you collect less revenue per dollar of tax base, and an economic effect, which holds that if you lower tax rates you get more economic growth and hence a larger tax base. Assessing which effect dominates, Laffer contends that the higher tax rates are before the cuts, the more likely it is that the economic effect will dominate.

Laffer's views were expounded in an interview in the *New York Times* on June 17, 1978. In national tax policy, Laffer favors cutting tax rates on the highest taxed income categories (for example, capital gains) and also those at the lowest end of the tax bracket. His preference in California would be a cut in progressive income taxes and a cut in sales taxes. Although he believes that Proposition 13 will benefit California by increasing employment and, in due course, by increasing revenue "quite substantially," Laffer says property tax cuts aren't as good as cuts in progressive income taxes and sales taxes but "They are better than nothing."

"I would much rather see full employment than very high spending on unemployment compensation," Laffer contends, putting a premium on expanding the tax base and then using those revenues for "very needed public services."

In essence, then, the conservative position says the free market will solve any disruptions in public services occasioned by tax cuts. More money in people's pockets will generate both consumer spending and business investment (including housing construction), thus creating a higher rate of economic growth. Income tax, sales tax and property tax *receipts* would thus rise, even though tax *rates* were at a lower level.

The difficulty economists have in knowing whether these theories are correct can be seen in the about face done by one group of economists in California. The month before the vote on Proposition 13, economists at the UCLA Graduate School of Management said its passage would mean the loss of up to 450,000 jobs in the state. A week after passage, the same group sharply revised its forecast. Taking into account revenues the state would transfer to localities, as well as increased consumer income, the economists now said the net impact of the property tax cuts "will be positive."

GREATER STATE CONTROL

There is no question that the passage of Proposition 13 will point California in the direction of greater state, and possibly also federal control of schools. Chapter 3 portrayed California school districts passing the buck after the Jarvis Initiative vote to Sacramento, as manifested by their waiting for the legislature to come up with funds to bail them out of their budget dilemmas. The legislature's voting of funds did provide *immediate* relief to school districts and municipalities but it also promised to greatly increase state control of public education.

This development immediately provoked thoughtful commentary, the most eloquent of which came from Richard P. Nathan, a senior fellow at the Brookings Institution and head of the Institution's Monitoring Studies Group to assess the impact of federal grant programs. Nathan, tracing the steady decline of the property tax as a percent of all local revenue in the past several decades, which, as noted in the June 8, 1978 *Wall Street Journal*, fell from 42.9% in 1950 to 30.8% in 1976, pointed out that the affirmative vote on Proposition 13 could lower this proportion to close to 25%. Since the property tax is the main local tax, Nathan said the implication for "increased dependence of local governments for sustenance from on high" was clear.

"The question is how far we want to go in relying on state revenues and the consequent impact the state would have in policy making," Nathan said in an interview, noting that "The financial question is connected to the political question of local control, which is a tradition that goes back hundreds of years." Going beyond the immediate impact of the Proposition 13 vote in California, Nathan conceded he would look at what other states do "and if I projected that Jarvis-Gann would produce a particularly low ratio of local funding in California, I would want to see alternatives to local revenues." Stating that the California situation has been rife with emotionalism, Nathan suggested, "We have to think intelligently about it, think about whether we shouldn't shift tax resources as they do in Maryland with a piggyback tax where . . . 20% of the personal income taxes collected are handed over to local government and a penny of the state sales tax." In Nathan's view, "Those are the kinds of things people should learn about and look at."

The situation in California, and the Proposition 13 vote, do not represent a blueprint for taxpayer revolts in other states, according to Nathan. He called the California situation unique because of the four factors at work: high property taxes, rapid increases in those taxes, a state surplus and the existence of the referendum process for amending the state constitution, something which only 13 other states have.

CUTTING PROPERTY TAXES, INCREASING OTHER TAXES

Lowering property taxes and maintaining even a minimum level of services means raising taxes elsewhere. Alternatives to the property tax are varied, ranging from suggestions such as Harrington's reliance on a "radically reformed income tax" to increases in charges of various types. In an interview, Arnold Meltsner of the School of Public Policy at the University of California/Berkeley, said he expects an increase in charges, i.e. anything a city or local government can put a charge on, resulting from passage of Proposition 13. As examples, he envisions charges on use of facilities which are now free (golf courses, swimming pools, highways) as well as a possible increase in the transit fare (transit fares were raised in Los Angeles and San Francisco soon after the June 6 vote, and increases appeared likely in other California cities as well). According to Meltsner, charges will be levied in areas which are within the discretion of local governments, because charges on these can be imposed without voter approval. For example, the Santa Ana Fire Department said in mid-June 1978 that it was thinking about charging a $1 monthly fee to households that wanted to subscribe to its paramedic emergency service; nonsubscribers would have to come up with $50 for each paramedic call.

On the state level, Meltsner feels there may also be more reliance on sales and income taxes, with funds from these sources then being channeled to local governments which are losing property tax revenues. States may also increase the rate structure and yield of their taxes and tax items not previously taxed. For example, taxes could be raised on cigarettes and/or liquor, depending on the state itself and its history and attitudes to such items. Depending on the anti-business bias in a given state, taxes could also be levied on inventories or general gross receipts, depending again on what taxes are already imposed.

Reviewing Tax Structures

Essentially, states will have to review their tax structure and increase those taxes already imposed as well as look for other ways to raise money.

In the entire area of state vs. local control over taxes and the flow of funds for essential services, it is important to note that the local mandate in California was lost because government was not responsive to a growing desire to keep budgets down or to permit only moderate increases. There are those, like Allan Odden, director of the Education Finance Center at the Education Commission of the States, who wondered in an interview "Why did it have to come to Jarvis?" Essentially, Odden says, the Jarvis Initiative triumphed because problems were not expressed and solved locally. Overburdened taxpayers eventually used the forum of a statewide referendum to vent their spleen over a situation which they felt, harking back to the days of the Boston Tea Party and the Revolutionary war, was taxation without representation.

One long-term solution, favored by Odden, would see the state take over *some* essential services. This could involve education, welfare and the courts, with other services, such as fire, police, sanitation, etc. left to local governments to support by the property tax. This would involve a basic shift in the level of government that funds local functions. School districts, for example, which have traditionally relied on the local property tax for the bulk of their education dollars would turn instead to the state for such funding, putting their property tax revenues into local services other than education. As noted in Chapter 4, states like Iowa and Minnesota which have reformed their property tax systems have already boosted state support for education significantly.

Business Taxes

Another solution would be to increase various taxes levied on the business sector of the community. A hard pill to swallow for Californians has been the fact that passage of Proposition 13 gave a $4.5 billion property tax reduction to businesses. One proposal offered in the California legislature in June 1978 would have amended Proposition 13 through a new constitutional amendment retaining the 1% tax limit on residential property but restoring previous tax rates on commercial property. Such a proposal would have to go to the voters.

Still another solution, one mentioned in Chapter 4, would be for states to take action effecting property tax relief before taxpayers revolted. An example would be the property tax freeze instituted in Indiana in 1973. Since this means increases in education are funded not by local government but by the state, it involves a letting go of a certain amount of local control over public schools.

Odden underscored one feeling that politicians may find hard to accept but which was richly manifested in the June 6 vote in California: "The reality may be that people don't want to spend anymore, and if the people feel this way, this must be accepted."

IMPROVING THE EFFECTIVENESS OF EDUCATION

Chapter 3 provided an overview of the dilemma in which 20 California school districts found themselves as a result of passage of Proposition 13. How well the districts cope inevitably will depend on the resourcefulness and skill of the leaders and staff in each local school system.

Educators around the country who were interviewed for this book (see Chapter 6) make a persuasive case that only by maintaining an "open door" toward district voters can a school system attract community support for budgets and programs. In a sense, the two-to-one passage of Proposition 13 in California can be seen as a vote against the "closed door" policy of government which continued to raise taxes (and stow away a burgeoning surplus) despite clear signs of taxpayer dissatisfaction and pending revolt.

There has been great dissatisfaction with public schools in the 1970s for a variety of reasons: alleged failure to teach the "basics," inability to deal with discipline problems and what has been perceived as a growing generation of functional illiterates. Not all of these charges are necessarily substantiated by fact. Nevertheless, inasmuch as they are believed by the taxpayers who provide much of the dollars for school funding they must be dealt with by school districts.

The movement for competency based education, which calls for students to meet minimum standards before being promoted to the next grade or graduated from high school, is a reaction to parental feeling that the schools are failing to educate children properly. Since 1975, 33 states have either passed laws or promulgated administrative rulings to this effect, among them Florida, Maryland and New Jersey. Educators can offer some evidence that school standards have not really fallen, including comparisons of pupil performance on standardized tests given today with performance of 20 or 30 years ago. But since the failures of the schools are both more visible and much more numerous than in the past, if only because school population has risen over 20 years, it is not enough for educators to hide behind ambiguous statistics. There are enough shortcomings of the schools that administrators can't afford to be trapped into a blind defense that says they're doing the best they can, and that any failings belong to society at large.

In a sense, the vote on Proposition 13 can be seen as a mandate to improve the value received from tax dollars spent on education as well as a mandate to lower property taxes. There can be positive effects to schools from the vote on the Jarvis Initiative. One could be an excuse to consolidate underutilized facilities, and to step up such efforts where they were lagging. An example of this could be the decision of the Pasadena School District to change its four-level school system to a three-level system, consolidating grades 7 and 8 with an elementary portion of the system.

Another benefit could be financial re-evaluation of staffing patterns. The number of teachers has actually continued to rise about 2% annually despite declining enrollments in the 1970s: the number of kindergarten through 12th grade teachers in 1975-76 was 2.2 million compared to 2.0 million in 1970-71, despite a 2.4% decline in enrollment in that period.

Third, tax reform could force reduction in administrative expenses. Assuming that schools which have to make cutbacks will cut bricks and mortar first, people second and program third, there may have to be terminations and demotions for administrative personnel as well as for teachers and non-teaching employees.

These rearrangements may be painful for school districts and their employees, just as belt-tightening by corporations competing in declining markets may be difficult. But there is nothing that says that taking these steps will not result in a stronger, more effective public education system in the long run.

6
The Next 90 Days, The Next Year

A property tax revolt is the stuff of news magazine covers, of television network specials, of expressions of concern or artful equivocation by politicians. And in fact, the week after California's vote on Proposition 13, the covers of *Time* and *Newsweek* depicted enthusiastic citizens hoisting the placards of protest, while the inside pages were filled with comparisons to the Boston Tea Party. CBS and NBC rushed to air specials on the revolt. Sensing a sea change, politicians have dropped anchor and retired to read the weather charts. Elected officials, asked for statements to include in this book, were uncharacteristically reticent. When new winds of uncertain force and direction are blowing, it's best not to be caught with too much sail exposed.

But how real is the tax revolt and what does it portend for the nation's schools?

Interviews conducted with scores of educators and school board members from all parts of the country immediately after the June 6 success of Proposition 13 revealed a calmer situation. No one was panicking, because conditions vary from one locality to another, and because in many parts of the country, educators have been under siege for half a dozen years already.

The first point, so often overlooked, is vital to keep in

mind. Education is a state responsibility under the U.S. Constitution, and a local function by custom. There are still more than 16,000 operating school districts in the U.S., including more than 6500 that enroll 1000 or more pupils. Federal legislation forbids the federal government from exercising control over the curriculum or textbooks used in local schools; states can and do impose a bewildering array of requirements, but there is little uniformity. The sheer unmanageability of education from a national viewpoint has always been a curse and a blessing: a curse when it comes to adopting some universal good, such as better science instruction; a blessing when it comes to resisting some dreaded scourge, like an army of budget cutters raising axes to the schoolhouse door.

THE LOCAL PERSPECTIVE

Of course, national trends do intrude, and sometimes they dominate. A relaxed superintendent ("Would you believe I'm talking to you on a Mickey Mouse phone?" he said) in the upstate New York town of Williamsville, outside Buffalo, put it this way: "A lot of time you're affected by the national publicity, it has a carryover to the local district."

The superintendent, A. Bernard Hatch, recalled the vote a couple of years ago when voters were being asked to spend about $1 million for 42 new school buses. A well publicized school bus accident in California had recently been in the news, and to Hatch's astonishment, the expenditure was approved easily.

But Hatch still believes that local mood, local facts, local sentiment in the end determine the degree of local support for the schools, and he has a strong record of getting his budgets passed.

The key, he says, is making the citizens feel "that they can come in and get an answer to a question at any time. If someone wants information, they can walk right in and if it's a tough question, put it right to me. That's the atmosphere that creates the best atmosphere for a budget vote."

If this seems like a suburban prescription for school harmony, it is. Williamsville in 1977-78 spent $29 million to educate its 12,000 pupils, which works out to nearly $2500 per child – far above the national average, and high even for New York State. "We have one of the higher per capita expenditures in the area," Hatch says. "We believe we're one of the better school districts in the area. Our attitude is, 'yeah, we can do it cheaper, if you'll accept that kind of program.' "

(Whether it was because of local sentiment or the spill-over from national news, however, Williamsville had a tough time with its proposed 1978-79 budget, which had sought a $1.8 million increase. On June 14, 1978, the voters turned it down by a five to one margin.)

Beaverton's Approach

Across the country in Beaverton, Oregon, one of that state's largest districts, a similar open door policy has pro-duced wide support for school programs. Boyd Applegarth, the superintendent, described the district's extensive volun-teer program – more than 2500 volunteers for a district of 20,500 pupils – its lay budget committee and its system of "local school committees" that advise the board of the needs of particular schools. Pat Ross, the school board president, recalls that two years ago the voters said no to a tax levy three times. That led to a shakeup of budgeting procedures, including establishment of a citizens committee of 14 people that goes out on school visits with the seven-member board.

One effect has been a study of central administration that led to a reorganization and reduction of administrative personnel from a high of 102 to a level of about 85.

Even though property rolls in Beaverton are increasing year by year, making possible small reductions in the tax rate, "We're beginning to hear the rumblings" from the California vote, says Applegarth, referring to the initiative circulating in Oregon to limit the property tax to 1.5% of market value. Speaking of the taxpayer revolt, Ross says "My feeling is that it's really based on emotion a lot more than reason. People are not thinking through the consequences . . . they don't trust what the politicians are telling them."

Fed Up With Taxes

Again and again the theme cropped up in our interviews that school budgets run into trouble because they're one of the few tax bills that citizens actually get to vote on. In Tempe, Arizona, where tax rates are amazingly low by New York or California standards, the voters can still object. This happened May 16, 1978 when they turned down a proposal to increase the budget by $839,000. The rejection meant eliminating 17 teaching positions and cancelling a 3% pay raise. It was the first such vote that Tempe had ever lost, and the margin was convincing: two to one. Robert Curry, associate superintendent, explained, "People are fed up with taxes. And the thing they can vote on is city or school taxes."

The superintendent in Pontiac, Michigan, Dana Whitmer, had a similar perspective. Interviewed on June 13, he explained that voters the day before had denied a request for an increase in the operating levy of $5.45 per $1000 of assessed valuation (see Chapter 4). Whitmer sees no sudden groundswell of tax cutting in the wake of the California vote, just "a pervasive feeling that the 'politicans' are free and loose with the money." In Pontiac, as elsewhere, cutting the budget inevitably means trimming the staff: about 60 teachers out of a staff exceeding 1000 will have to go, most of them by attrition rather than layoffs.

Then there are the districts that have grown so used to adversity they don't remember anything else. Thomas Van Dam, superintendent of District 151 in South Holland, Illinois, speaks the way Job might if he were reincarnated as a school administrator. District 151 went through forced desegregation in 1968 and never recovered; parents of a thousand white students pulled their kids out of the public schools (enrollment is now 1200, down from a peak of 2600). They have been saying no to increased tax levies ever since: a dozen no votes in the past 10 years. "Proposition 13 doesn't mean a thing here," says a battleweary Van Dam. "We've been living on borrowing money from future taxes since the sixties." Having given up on building community support for school programs, District 151 has become adept at attracting federal and state grants, which supply 22% of its $3 million budget.

BIG CITY PROBLEMS

In some ways the big cities have advantages over smaller districts, because there's rarely a vote on the school budget per se, and city property tax rates are frequently lower than in the suburbs. But when cities, especially older Northern cities, get into a financial jam, the school systems have bruises to show. It happened in New York City in 1976, when near bankruptcy caused a loss of jobs for thousands of school employees. In Philadelphia in 1977 the schools were so close to insolvency that they needed an emergency loan to stay open.

One city superintendent who has tapped an astonishing degree of community support is M. Donald Thomas of Salt Lake City. Voters there in the past five years have passed a nine mill increase in the tax levy by a 70% margin; the vote in favor of a $40 million bond measure was 67%. Thomas attributes the support to what he calls "shared governance," a commitment by the board and administration to community participation. The tangible signs are a comprehensive volunteer program, strong business involvement (companies like IBM, Mountain Bell, Utah Power & Light have "adopted" schools, taking students as interns and sending their employees into the schools to teach) and an open door policy to the local news media.

But how typical is Salt Lake City? The homogeneous Mormon community, the rising tax rolls as new business moves in, and above all, the relatively small size of the school system — about 23,000 pupils — suggest that it is not very typical. Shared governance may be fine for Salt Lake City, but in New York City the school system was "decentralized" after bruising battles over community control in the late 1960s, and today, the percentage of voter turnout in elections for local boards is 7%.

The real problem suggested by Proposition 13 in California, and similar initiatives offered in other states is not the revenue loss they threaten. Even California school districts will somehow weather the next year, through a combination of state aid, program cutbacks and higher local taxes for those districts that can muster the necessary two thirds majority.

THE CRISIS OF CONFIDENCE

The long-run problem is that the tax cutting movement bespeaks a loss of confidence that makes it particularly difficult for the public schools to do their job, and to succeed at it. Loss of confidence afflicts all public services, from the massive federal bureaucracy handling Medicare or income taxes to the tens of thousands of city halls and town halls around the country giving out recreational permits and fishing licenses. But most public services are one way in nature. It requires no public confidence for the sanitation workers to do their job: they pick up the garbage and don't much care if citizens have nice things to say about them as they bang around the garbage cans.

But the process of education is far more subtle. The reason it's easier to teach school in Scarsdale, New York and Beaverton, Oregon than in Cleveland or Philadelphia is that the parents in Scarsdale and Beaverton reinforce what the schools are doing in so many ways: by the way they speak, by the informal education that they transmit to their children, by the examples of career success that follows success in school, and of course, by direct exhortation to do homework and attend to lessons.

If schools forfeit that confidence, if they lose their natural constituency of well-educated parents who approve of what the schools are doing and who vote to give them the needed funds, then the long-range prospects for public education are poor indeed. This is why some educators are willing to state frankly that California's vote on Proposition 13 isn't all bad, that its shock value has some beneficial aspects.

One such educator is Carl Marburger, formerly the state education commissioner in New Jersey and now with an organization called The National Committee for Citizens in Education in Columbia, Maryland. Through publications such as *The Rights of Parents*, NCCE has hammered away at a few themes: that parents have a right and duty to be involved in school decisions, that they are legally entitled to information about school performance and programs, that improvement in the schools won't happen without community involvement.

Catastrophe Provides Opportunity

Marburger's reaction to the present crisis is succinct: "Catastrophe provides opportunity." What the budget-cutting votes say to educators, he explains is "Hey, we've got to take a look at the sacred cows . . . We're going to do some serious pruning and cutting and there are a lot of ways we could trim back our sails." Marburger mentions ideas such as year-round schools or other ways of organizing schools. He argues that tenure should be re-examined and that increases in class size may not be all bad. "Twenty four kids per class isn't sacred. Perhaps I'd hit hard at keeping it as low as possible in kindergarten or first grade." After that point, he notes, research doesn't support the contention that smaller class size helps learning "unless it gets to a certain point — if you have 50 kids in a class you'll have chaos."

Bernard Haake, superintendent of schools of the Chappaqua, New York Public Schools, makes a similar point. "A large part of our operation is baby sitting. Another part of it is sophisticated, expert instruction. Not everything has to be done 25 to one. You can get 300 kids together for music. You can put 150 kids in a typing class. Other things have to be done one to one."

Haake also observes that "There's a lot of technology around now that can help," including home computers selling for $600 and under. The point is seconded by Howard Hitchens, executive director of the Association for Educational Communications and Technology in Washington, D.C. He notes that when bad winter weather shut down schools in Columbus, Ohio, innovative use of television managed to get lessons to many thousands of youngsters.

Haake sees the votes around the country as a message to all public servants that "We're pretty unresponsive at all levels." The irony is that the schools, which may be a bit more responsive than other agencies, are "going to get clobbered" the worst. Taxpayers don't vote on the appropriation for the Defense Department, the state highway department or the local recreation department. They do vote on spending for the schools. As one educator interviewed for this report put it, "Let me know when the initiative comes along on federal taxes. That's the crusade I'm signing up for."

A surprising number of administrators regarded the tax revolt as a movement that might produce some eventual benefits for the public schools, e.g., by focusing public attention better on what to emphasize. Said Dana Whitmer from Pontiac, "We're going to have some turmoil . . . But it may be that as a result, there'll be a fundamental reevaluation of public education, a balance between public support and what professionals think should happen."

Even superintendents who talk about the desirability of public participation in educational policymaking concede that the process can be terribly time-consuming, with its endless task forces, committee meetings, group reports, visits. An acute budget crisis can have the effect of telescoping the process.

The Dark Side

For every educator who can discern a glimmer of good in the taxpayer revolt, there's another who sees the dark side. Larry Cuban, superintendent of the Arlington, Virginia Public Schools, puts it this way: "If [the tax cutting fever] springs from a kind of general anger at government, there are going to be lots of negative results." School systems, he argued, are very vulnerable to such emotional movements and to politicians "pandering to the feeling that government is bloated." By implication, he argues, why should the schools suffer if they've done a good job? Affluent Arlington spends about $2700 a year to educate its students, and according to Cuban, "Parent support for the school system is extremely high."

WHO GETS HURT

One of the most pertinent questions is, who gets hurt most when the budget cutting begins in earnest? If all groups involved in the educational enterprise dig in their heels to protect professional prerogatives or job security at all cost, the result will be a knockdown battle to cut out the other fellow's programs. Some administrators saw in the current crisis the possibility that teachers' unions would get their comeuppance. Others complained of the burden of all the mandated programs forced on them by state legislatures in recent years — education of the handicapped, bilingual programs — suggesting there would be welcome pressure to jettison these costlier activities in favor of basic instruction. The California districts which moved quickly to shut down their summer schools undoubtedly were responding to a common sentiment: protect the three R's for the largest number of pupils, discard what serves only the minority.

Administrators like Bernard Haake of Chappaqua would argue that the time of greatest crisis is the moment to appeal to all of the interest groups concerned with education. He rejects the idea of ramming desired innovations like differentiated staffing or altered schedules down the throats of the teachers. "You don't really make changes in education unless the practitioners are involved. Our budget is 80% personnel costs ... We can't change procedures unless the teachers union sees a self interest in changing."

Unfortunately for those who still believe that effective control of the schools must reside locally, one inevitable consequence of the tax cutting mood will be to weaken, not strengthen, local control. This was a nearly universal feeling of both administrators and independent experts interviewed for this report. When voters reject the property tax for school support, other taxes must come into play, taxes that in many cases only state governments can levy. Localities in California turned immediately to the state for help; the consequences of the state's putting up an additional $2 billion or more for education are that a bit more power over educational decisions will flow toward Sacramento.

In New York in May 1978, when the state court of appeals ruled that local districts could not exceed constitutional property tax limitations for certain educational costs, the districts had nowhere to turn but to Albany. The state legislature came through with an emergency package of grants and loans: once again the same pattern. Having fallen from 53% to 47% in 10 years, the proportion of school costs footed by local taxes is destined to fall even further.

Though the National Education Association and other groups will continue their clamor for a bigger federal share of education costs, there is little discernible support for this position in Washington. The week after the vote on Proposition 13 in California, the House of Representatives voted to lop $1 billion from the appropriation for the Department of Health, Education and Welfare, the saving to come from elimination of "waste." Until politicians have a better idea how far the tide of tax resentment may rise, they are not going to swim against it with bold new federal spending plans.

The action in educational finance will continue to be at the state level, with rich districts battling poorer ones, cities tangling with suburbs, over complex equalization and state aid formulas. And for the legislature that gives in too fully to the blandishments of any single constituency, there is always the threat of court suits like the famous Serrano V. Priest in California* to restore a semblance of equity.

---

*In that case a California court ordered the state to find ways of providing more equal per-pupil expenditures than were available through the property tax.

CHOICES FOR VOTERS AND CITIZENS

Even if an inevitable consequence of the present crisis will be a further shift of control over education to the states, local voters will still make many of the important decisions about education. The movement to cut or limit property taxes is a grass roots one that took many politicians by surprise. It remains for citizens in each local community to make their own choices about the proper balance between taxes and public services, especially educational services.

Citizens will want to put the following questions to themselves in making these choices:

1. What are the strengths and weaknesses of the local school system? How clearly has the community spelled out the aims of the system?

2. How fully has the school board invited participation from all the groups that could contribute to better school programs: parents, teachers, pupils, local employers?

3. Have alternative ways of allocating the school budget been considered, including closing or consolidating schools, reorganizing staff or cutting programs that appeal to a small minority of pupils?

4. Has the cost of operating the system been compared to costs for districts of similar size and wealth in the area, and in other parts of the country?

5. Has the district taken full advantage of available state and federal aid programs?

Some of these questions may seem to prejudge matters, e.g., by suggesting that schools should be closed or staff reorganized or cut. But unless those disposed to support the schools can discipline themselves to look at their school system dispassionately, the budget will be open to attack from individuals not favorably disposed to education, whose criterion is not, "How can we do the best job of education at a price the community can afford?" but "How can we cut taxes to the maximum degree?"

These are difficult days for public education. As this book has shown, movements to limit or reduce taxes are underway in several dozen states across the nation. The effect of the amendment already passed in California will be painful readjustment, loss of jobs and contraction of programs on the part of many school districts. No one involved in education can take for granted that local school systems will retain their present shape now that new forces have been loosed.

Yet this book has shown that the taxpayer revolt is far from a monolithic nationwide crusade. The extreme cuts in public spending brought about by California's vote were largely the product of special circumstances, not a harbinger of what is to occur elsewhere. In some states, reform of the tax structure supporting education has already proceeded quite far. In other areas of the country, sentiment is more for holding the line on taxes and spending than it is for wholesale cutbacks in public services.

The lesson for all those concerned with education is still a somber one. Educators have argued among themselves for years about what the demand for "accountability" means. Is it school boards that are to be held accountable? Principals? Teachers? Citizen votes on tax limitation measures and on local school budgets are a brusque reminder that in the end, all who are engaged in public education are accountable to those who pay the bills.

The value of the taxpayer revolt is not that it will put some final limit on what can be spent on public services in general and the schools in particular. Imposing such limits is often simplistic or wrong headed. (It would be ironic if a host of states were to enact rigid controls on increases in local education budgets by the early 1980s — just when school enrollments should begin climbing again.) Rather, the value of the crisis is in stimulating those involved in education to consider what are the most urgent tasks of schooling, and how scarce resources can be allocated to achieve them. Out of such consideration may come a new consensus on how to preserve and ultimately enrich the schools that educate America's children.

7
Reactions:
Statements About the Crisis from
National Leaders and Organizations

President Jimmy Carter
Statements at Press Conference of June 14, 1978

Q. Mr. President, Proposition 13 could appear to have sent some politicians into shock, including some in this town. You don't appear to be in shock, but I wonder if the California vote will have any influence on your possibly reassessing your own policies and approaches.

A. Obviously, we will have to observe carefully the developments in California in the future, as the full impact of Proposition 13 is felt. It will reduce property taxes perhaps as much as 60 percent in California. One of the reasons for the decision made by the citizens of California is that property taxes there are very high compared to those in other parts of the nation — most other parts of the nation. The property valuations have increased rapidly and the taxes levied have increased rapidly.

That, combined with the well known fact that the state government had accumulated $4.5 or $5 billion or so in surplus funds, I think combined to increase the desire of California people to impose this limit on property taxes.

Those factors would be unlikely to prevail in other states of the nation at this time. But the 2-to-1 margin of approval by the California people to restrain public spending and taxation is obviously a message that's been well received and observed by all of us throughout the country.

I think this is not incompatible with the fact that we want to hold down spending, we want to reduce taxes at the federal government level. There will be some indirect impact on the federal government and more direct influence in the future because there's no doubt about the fact that unemployment will go up in California as government workers are laid off because of stringent budget requirements and, of course, our unemployment compensation payments will have to increase.

Also, I think we have about 50,000 CETA jobs — Comprehensive Education Training Administration jobs, worked out jointly with local governments. Many of those may be in danger.

We have no way yet to anticipate what other consequences will accrue. But all of us are concerned about the budget levels, about unnecessary spending, about more efficient operation of government and about lower taxation. These were proposals that have already been made by us here in Washington. But I think they strengthen support now in the Congress for those considerations.

Q. Mr. President, to get back to Proposition 13, sir, today Budget Director McIntyre called it wishful thinking to suggest that communities in California could ask the federal government to bail them out of difficulties with their local payrolls, etc. There was an indication that he was speaking for you on this. Was he, and how do you feel about that and if you were to get such requests from localities what would you tell them?

A. Well, within the constraints of the presently existing programs for transportation, education, for air and water pollution control, crime control under L.E.A.A., CETA jobs for public service and training, of course we would be glad to help the communities of California on the same basis as we help communities around the country. And if there should evolve a crisis in a community, after careful assessment within the bounds of the law and administrative procedures we would obviously help them.

The federal impact of the California decision will be felt long in the future. I think with a $5 billion surplus that presently exists in the state government for several months in the future this can be used, as Governor Brown has very wisely proposed, to deal with those special needs.

Following that time, of course, we'll have to assess what role the federal government might play. But I don't think there would be any possibility of our passing a specific law just to deal with California. The reason for the interrelation on taxes, for instance, is to prevent double taxation. And I think even with the reduced taxes on property in California — the taxes, for instance, in states like Georgia or Alabama — would still be quite a lot lower than those in California.

So we still have no means nor inclination to single out California for special federal programs just because they have lowered property taxes.

Joseph A. Califano, Secretary, Department of Health, Education and Welfare Statement at Press Conference, June 20, 1978

My own judgment with respect to Proposition 13 is that it reflects some very particular problems in California. The property taxes are higher than in many other states. There has been a lot of discussion of "no growth" and what have you. I do not believe that the American people want a situation where Johnny can't read simply because the school door is closed. I think they want Johnny to read. But I think they want school programs administered effectively and efficiently. I think they want to wring out the waste, fraud and abuse in these programs.

Gov. Edmund G. (Jerry) Brown Jr.
Address Before Joint Session of California Legislature
June 8, 1978

Mr. Speaker, Mr. Senate Pro Tem, Members of the Legislature, friends, visitors, people of California.

Over 4 million of our fellow citizens have sent a message to City Hall, Sacramento, and to all of us. The message is that the property tax must be sharply curtailed and that government spending, wherever it is, must be held in check. We must look forward to lean and frugal budgets. It is a great challenge and we will meet it. We must do everything possible to minimize the human hardship and maximize the total number of state jobs created in our economy. Proposition 13 takes place on July 1. We have only three weeks to act — three weeks to decide multi-billion dollars of fiscal questions; to set a new direction for the five thousand units of government throughout our state. It is time to put aside partisan differences. The vote represented Democrats, Republicans, people from the north and the south, old and young in all parts of our wonderful state. We must follow three basic principles — no new state taxes. Voters have told us they want a tax cut, they don't want a shell game.

No. 2. The state must share the burden. We must adopt a thoughtful, austere budget. Already I have imposed a hiring freeze. There will be no new hiring and when someone leaves state service he or she will not be replaced unless it is an emergency or unless there is extraordinary reason. We must keep the uncertainty to a minimum.

I will propose budget cuts of at least $300 million. The more money we can save at the state level the more we can share with local governments, fire, police, schools, cities, counties and all those who carry out the people's wish. During the next several days, no later than the next two to three weeks, I will recommend legislation to accomplish six specific tasks.

No. 1. A law is needed to allocate the remaining property tax, that which is left after the 1% limit now imposed by Proposition 13.

No. 2. We must commit the entire state surplus to meet the urgent needs of our public schools and local governments. I recommend for this year, and this year only, $4 billion in direct aid and $1 billion in an emergency loan fund. I recommend this for the first year because of the uncertainties that local government will face. Loan money must be made available so that the budgets that will be formed in the next few weeks can be written with as much dispatch and human compassion as we know how to make it. The current surplus is not ongoing. It has been built up out of tight fiscal management here in Sacramento and by a booming state economy.

For the following year we should have approximately $2 billion to share with local governments and with the funds that will be returned from the loan fund we can make, hopefully, another billion dollars available to share with local governments in the very difficult and painful transition. We need a temporary one-year formula for allocating the surplus where it is most needed. There is no time in the next three weeks for a comprehensive overhaul of a series of complex formulas. We need a bill that commends itself to two thirds of the people in these Chambers, Republicans and Democrats, and we need it soon. People across the state are looking to us for leadership.

Should we need a special contingency fund for emergency situations, we need that because no matter what the formula is, and especially if it is simple, there will be arbitrary impact and we must be able to meet them. The $1 billion emergency loan fund must be established so that the traditional units of local government can meet their cash flow needs that in some cases will be coming due in the next couple of weeks.

Finally, the legislature itself must adopt a lean and frugal state budget. Certainly that is the message which we hear and to the extent that we do that we not only respond to the people's will but we share with all the people of the state at whatever level of government the very difficult challenge that faces us ahead.

After July 1 I will offer additional suggestions. Plans to limit government spending, examining and overhauling the confusing local jurisdictions, the special districts that now dot our state to the number of over 5000. I will ask the federal government to reexamine its priorities. Now, when property taxes are cut, the federal government will enjoy a $2 billion windfall. The incentive should be the other way around. Where people have spoken to protect their homes the federal government should assist not by reaping a windfall but by providing assistance to those who face troubled times here in state government.

Finally, a very important point. There are many hard-working people in state and local government. They are not faceless bureaucrats, they have families, they pay taxes, they have the same lives as all the rest of us, and they have to also make plans for their future and for that reason I appeal to you to rise above the partisan temptations, to work together as a body, to fashion a bill that keeps faith with our fiscal realities and with the mood and the philosophy of the people which we serve. Major human tragedies will occur unless we do all that we can, unless we continuously scrutinize every element of our budget, every possibility of our surplus and lay out a plan that will carry us through this first year of transition and will provide opportunities in the second year and beyond to smooth the path for an orderly government both at the state level and at local levels.

As for business, business will reap savings in the order of

$3 billion. Many individual businesses will save tens of millions of dollars. These people, these corporate presidents, have a moral obligation to invest that money in California, to create jobs, to create the possibilities of a continuing boom and buoyant economy. It is only through that method will we be able to shelter and smooth the shock in the disruption that can occur.

We have a very monumental task. There is not much time. The people are waiting for us to act.

Thank you very much.

Wilson Riles, California State Superintendent of Public Instruction

Statement to Joint Legislative Conference Committee on Senate Bill 154, June 14, 1978

Gentlemen:

I gratefully appreciate this opportunity to outline my position regarding the legislative steps that need to be taken in elementary and secondary education to implement Proposition 13. I share with you a broad concern for the quality of life in California and I understand the immense difficulty of trying to balance a $7 billion loss in local revenue with the $5 billion available in state surplus. This is compounded by the equally complex responsibility to make judgments regarding the relative needs of the public schools, police and fire protection, public health, libraries, parks and recreation and a host of other local services.

The task before us is to set out a careful and deliberate course of action which will respond to the immediate revenue crisis in a simple, straightforward manner. We should also consciously avoid determining major policy decisions which can be more systematically dealt with at the next legislative session. In the next few weeks we have neither the time nor the level of public involvement necessary to make long term decisions about our public schools. I believe that the public should be meaningfully involved in any major decision affecting the education of their youngsters.

A recent poll revealed that if cuts were to be made in public services that 82% of these polled would prefer that they be made in areas other than education. Nevertheless, we all know there must be reduction and education must assume its share.

I will outline today both a short term approach which will respond to the current school district revenue crisis and a long term approach for determining future educational policy directions.

It is important to recognize that schools have been making reductions and foregoing improvements to ease the statewide burden of property taxes longer than other elements of local government.

In 1972 tax rate limits were replaced by stringent revenue limits and expenditure controls. As a result, the growth in school revenues was less than the rate of inflation. Since that time AB 65 enacted during the last legislative session further refined this concept of revenue limits.

Recognizing this ongoing concern for the needs of the tax payer, we were still able to establish in AB 65 a school funding system which provides for a base responsive to the requirements of the Serrano decision, incentives for school improvement and categorical aids to respond to the needs of the handicapped, disadvantaged and the limited and non-English speaking. This framework for educational support can and should be preserved and I believe that my recommendations can be accomplished.

I propose in the short run:

1. That all elementary and secondary school districts,

county offices of education, special state-funded education programs, and the State Department of Education should share in any reduction of support.

2. State relief for schools should be apportioned with some regard for reducing disparities in expenditures among districts. However, in no instance should any district incur greater than a 15% reduction.

In particular, I propose that district spending at or below the foundation program level established in AB 65 assume a 6% reduction in anticipated support. For districts whose expenditures exceed the foundation level, I recommend that reductions be applied on a sliding scale with a maximum reduction of 15% applied to districts spending one and one-half times the foundation program or more.

3. That reductions be based on 1978-79 information and take into account the new apportionment provisions of AB 65.

4. Categorical programs, with restricted funding, should each assume an equal percentage reduction over levels previously established in AB 65.

These recommendations can be accomplished by the allocation of $2.2 billion of the state's surplus and would probably mean a total statewide cut of 10% for schools. I believe this to be a fair and equitable portion of the surplus for education and as much of a cut as we ought to ask our schools to assume. I have discussed my recommendations for the short term with members of the State Board of Education, school district representatives and the representatives of advisory groups and the large majority concur with my suggestions.

In the long run, I believe that the solution to the problems posed to schools by Proposition 13 must be resolved within the basic framework established by AB 65. We are not relieved of the responsibility to establish an equitable support system, nor should we diminish our commitment to seek quality education for all.

In the months ahead, I intend to work with the leadership of the legislature, members of the policy and finance committees, the administration and the State Board of Education to develop a plan for achieving broad public participation and input into the ultimate decisions regarding the future of education in this state.

In conclusion, this committee will face the hard problem of reconciling the many competing claims from within the educational community. I believe my plan transcends any special interest, it does not pit program versus program or district versus district. Furthermore, it is a fiscally realistic solution for our schools which recognizes the overall revenue shortfall created by Proposition 13.

Grace Baisinger, President, National PTA

Statement on School Finance and Proposition 13

A strong well-financed public school system is vital to the future health of our country. Yet the role of public education as the central democratizing institution in American life — "the balance wheel of society," in Horace Mann's words — is now being threatened by what is commonly referred to as the "taxpayers revolt."

Recently, taxpayers repeatedly defeated school bond referendums in Cleveland; overwhelmingly approved the Jarvis Amendment or Proposition 13 in California. Proposition 13 rolls back property taxes to 1% of 1975-76 assessed value and puts a lid on future expenditures by requiring a two thirds vote of the state legislature to raise state taxes to make up for the revenue lost by the roll back in property taxes and the support of two thirds of the electorate to increase local taxes. There is also support in Congress for a federal tuition tax credit for parents with children attending private elementary and secondary schools.

The "taxpayers revolt" has been characterized by many as an attack on public education; as dissatisfaction with public schools. We believe this is unfortunate. Nor is such an indictment supported by the facts.

While it is true that the consequences of Proposition 13 and tuition tax credits will result in less financial support for the public schools, and may very well be disastrous to public education as the equalizing force in American life, we do not believe that the efforts by taxpayers to secure some measure of relief from the tax burden should be construed as attacks on the public schools or as a loss of confidence in public education.

Indeed, despite the highly publicized "taxpayers revolt," results from the recently released survey by the National Opinion Research Center show that 41% of the public expressed a "great deal" of confidence in educators in 1977 (up from 31% in 1975). Furthermore, only 4% judged the public schools as being inadequate while police protection was rated inadequate by 8% and public transportation was found to be inadequate by 36%.

In the opinion of PTA, the "taxpayers revolt" is a cry from citizens everywhere to their state and federal governments to curb inflation. It is a plea to Congress to do something about genuine tax reform.

Nevertheless, we are deeply concerned about the domino effect of the California action to approve Proposition 13. The rush on the part of taxpayers throughout the country to find ways to limit spending and to roll back property taxes before they have an opportunity to study and understand the full implications of Proposition 13 is alarming.

Delegates at the National PTA convention in Atlanta, June 11-14, 1978, adopted a resolution directing the

National PTA to develop a plan of action to inform and educate its members as to the effects of Proposition 13, not only on the education of children and youth, but on the health and other services that are provided to children and their families, and other citizens as well.

Keeping in mind that some school districts in California have already announced that there would be no summer school programs for 1978, and that other programs and services would be cut drastically in the 1978-79 school year, PTAs everywhere will:

• Study carefully and seek to take part in the decision making which redirects existing school funds so that *optimum* use will be made of such funds.

• Seek alternative methods of school financing.

• Make known to the public that state and local tax cuts will increase dependence by counties, cities and local school districts on the federal government.

• Point out that with increasing dependence on the state and federal government for financial support, local control of education – a cherished American value – will diminish and erode.

In conclusion, the irony of such efforts as Proposition 13 to decrease property and state taxes is that approximately 25% of every dollar saved will end up in the federal treasury in the form of extra tax payments!

Albert Shanker, President
American Federation of Teachers
Statement of June 19, 1978

The lyrics of an old popular song said that love was sweeping the country. But judging from the comments since Californians voted 2-1 for Proposition 13 on their state ballot, we can expect instead a tidal wave of tax cut moves brought on by public resentment. Is it true? Does the California vote that slashed about $7 billion out of a total of $12 billion in local property taxes — a cut of roughly 58% — mean a general tax revolt all across the country? Just what does the victory of tax foes in California mean, for that state and for the nation? It's time to look at some of the effects and some of the assumptions.

First of all, Californians may wake up to find they have voted themselves an economic and social disaster. If the courts decide that Proposition 13 is constitutional, services provided by local government — schools, police, fire, libraries, hospitals, parks, sanitation — will have to be cut drastically. Workers will feel it, of course, through layoffs and the predictable assault on salaries and fringe benefits. But the public will suffer, too, through large-scale reductions in the things most Americans believe are basic and appropriate services of local government, including the education of children.

Second, Californians will not be saving as much as they think. While they have forced cuts in local revenues and services, the property tax cut is actually a boon to the federal government. Since property taxes are a deductible item on federal tax returns, Californians will no longer be able to deduct that amount which has been cut by Proposition 13. The federal tax bite on each taxpayer will be higher, and the federal government is likely to reap a tax windfall of some $2 billion.

There is real irony in this. Recent polls — including a

Gallup poll commissioned by *Newsweek* in the wake of the California vote and published in its issue dated June 19 — have shown that taxpayers believe they get the most value for their taxes from services performed by local government.

For example, while the *Newsweek* Gallup poll showed 57% in favor of a property tax cut, it also revealed that by even larger majorities Americans do *not* believe too many of their tax dollars are being spent on local services. Sixty-eight percent said their communities were spending "the right amount" or "too little" on public schools; there were majorities for most other services. When people in local communities across the land begin fully to understand that if they want these services, there must be tax dollars to pay for them, it is not likely they will vote their own versions of Proposition 13. The service cuts that are about to happen in California should provide a dramatic example for the rest of the country.

There is also reason to believe that the property values and property taxes in California that led to a revolt, while not unique, are certainly unusual. The rapid escalation of real estate prices and taxes — both nearly doubling in a very short time — added enormously to the burden of homeowners already being squeezed by the general inflation. That is not true in the rest of the country. Nevertheless, there is a message for all of us, including public employees whose jobs and incomes are themselves dependent on an adequate level of tax revenues. Property values in California are grossly inflated in part because of an extreme housing shortage. That shortage, which also exists elsewhere, although to a lesser degree, is directly related to the virtual halt in new construction during the Nixon-Ford years with their high interest rates. The fight to have a decent housing program nationally shouldn't be left to the building trades. It is everyone's fight.

The California vote and the polls surrounding it have left an unclear message. They probably mean that government must examine its programs, seek to reduce waste and inefficiency, and take a hard look at grossly unpopular policies.

They undoubtedly reveal broad public dissatisfaction with continuing inflation and the need for better efforts to control it. But there is no evidence of a national trend toward severe tax cuts, despite media speculation along those lines. And there is strong evidence that the public wants to maintain a fairly high level of essential services.

John Ryor, President, National Education Association
Statement of June 8, 1978

NEA has proposed legislation which is now before the Congress for the financing of public schools. Our legislation calls for an expanded federal commitment to the public schools and at the same time provides aid to States and individual taxpayers. This measure, the Education Act of 1978, establishes national policy for assisting schools in financial stress, including those in California. The Education Act provides a start toward reducing the burden on the property owner, who is now required to foot the bill for as much as 75% to 80% of the costs of our schools.

A viable long-range solution to the financial crisis afflicting public schools must provide a balanced method of funding education, a system in which broad-based, less regressive taxes such as the federal income tax provide a full one-third of the costs of our nation's schools. These monies must be channeled directly into our school systems in a manner that sustains local control of the schools. Then, if state governments each provide another third of the cost, the local property owner's burden will be dramatically lightened from as much as 80% of the total cost to 33% – a fair share.

NEA will continue to fight for workable long-range solutions to the problem of funding education in this country, and we will continue to oppose brutal and repressive measures like Proposition 13.

NEA's affiliate in California, the California Teachers Association, representing 186,000 California Teachers, has announced its intention to file suit challenging the constitutionality of Proposition 13. If the measure is held valid by the courts, CTA has taken the official position that schools should not open in September unless the California state legislature has acted to provide adequate funding to offer students a full and meaningful education program. Should local districts choose to open schools anyway, in spite of legislative inaction to provide needed funding, CTA President Stephen Edwards has called upon those districts to offer a full educational program so long as the available funds hold out and then to close schools rather than turn them into concentration camps in which teachers might be forced to perform the role of keepers instead of instructors, or mere baby sitting centers in which teachers would be forced to watch rather than teach their students.

Thomas A. Shannon, Executive Director,
National School Boards Association

Statement: The Hapless Mischief of Jarvis-Gann

The Jarvis-Gann Initiative limiting property tax support for California public schools is hapless mischief. Its 2-to-1 win at the polls is a message for lawmakers and school people. But it is *not* an anti-school message. It is a tax message.

Any tax system must be structured in light of economic realities. As the economic situation changes, the tax system also must change. In order to ensure that the tax system is in synch with the economy, the executive and legislative branches must continually monitor the economy and develop changes to the tax system that will reflect changes in the

economy that stem from a variety of sources, such as inflation, devaluation, escalating labor costs in key industries,
and shortages of critical items, to mention but a few. In
California's case, residential housing costs up and down the
coast skyrocketed in the past few years, tripling and quadru-
pling in some cities. As the market price of housing increased,
so did the assessed valuation required to be pegged at 25% of
the market price. And the property tax bill to pay for public
school and other local governmental services is based on
assessed valuation.

In California, the Governor and the Legislature either did
not appreciate the importance of keeping the tax system in
balance with the economy or failed to provide effective
leadership in making the necessary tuning adjustments to the
tax system. When they finally did respond in a hurry-up
fashion, it was the old story of "a day late and a dollar
short." And it is the school districts and other local government units that must bear the brunt of this tragic lack of
understanding or leadership at the state level.

For school people in California, the task is two fold:

(1) They must assert leadership in influencing the executive and legislative branches:

• to come up immediately with sufficient "replacement
revenue" to offset any property tax loss that otherwise could
result in 1978-79 being the year of the "Great Fiscal Deba-
cle"; and,

• to restructure the tax system for the long run so that
the quality of education can continue to improve, which
indeed it must to equip California youth to survive and
prosper in the 21st century.

(2) They must protect local representative governance
of the public schools. This means that:

• school people must thwart any proposal to shift control of the public schools to the state level. The old saw
about control being exercised by the governmental level providing the funds is invalid in this context because there are no

"state" dollars — only "local" dollars. The source of the funds should not be confused with the distribution process. School people will have to be alert lest the California Legislature stumbles into a financing plan that would magnify the role of the state bureaucracy in governing the local public schools at the expense of local control of, and accountability for, public school governance and administration.

● In considering any retrenchment proposals, school boards must ensure that budget cuts do not make effective governance impossible. In essence, school district budget cuts that would slash away:

● administrative and secretarial assistance to school boards;

● written school board or district policy development;

● public relations counsel on school district programs;

● legal counsel for school boards; and,

● participation by school boards in state and national school board association educational and leadership programs;

would hobble school boards to such an extent that competent governance would be rendered a nullity.

Certainly school people have a responsibility in formulating budget cuts to minimize the impact upon the classroom's instructional program. But, school boards, committed to lay control of, and accountability for, local public education, cannot afford, under any circumstances, to make budget cuts in their own support services to the point where they could no longer properly perform their governance functions. If school boards cut their own hamstrings through injudicious budget reductions, local lay control of public education in California will die. And the anomaly is that the death of local school boards would occur at a time when lay leadership of the public schools would be most needed because the passage of Jarvis-Gann has signalled:

● the beginning of a period of extreme turbulence in public school operation brought on by school district staff demoralization and controversies over job rights;

• a total reappraisal of how public elementary and secondary education should be financed in California as the Governor and State Legislature cast about in political agony to rescue the instructional programs of the public schools from disaster; and,

• a renewed effort to increase public support for the public schools, without which no real progress in leading California out of the darkness of Jarvis-Gann could be made.

School board members, who alone in all public educational matters in California represent the people and are directly accountable to them, are best suited to assume a leading role in a trying post-Proposition 13 period. And that is why school boards should closely husband their governance resources and not take the axe to trim budgets out of panic or misguided political efforts to satisfy school employee unions by "sharing the hurt," thus making themselves impotent in governing their school districts during the "reconstruction period" following this dreaded victory for Messrs. Jarvis and Gann.

National Taxpayers Union
Statement by Grover Glenn Norquist,
Assistant Executive Director
June 1978

California's Proposition 13 mandates a drastic and permanent cut in local property taxes. And because over half of local spending goes to finance public education, Proposition 13's passage on June 6 will mean significant reductions in taxpayer support for public schools. This reduced spending need not, however, result in lowering the quality of education our children receive. Indeed, there is every reason to believe that the quality of education will improve as a consequence of Proposition 13.

The budget cuts necessitated by this amendment will focus public attention on the spending policies of public schools and school committees will be asked to identify their priorities. Unlike the education bureaucracy, parents and taxpayers have only one interest: to provide for their children the finest education possible for the least tax burden.

Political pressures created by Proposition 13 and other tax relief measures will bring the priorities of the "professional educators" in line with the priorities of the taxpayer/parent. The present lack of oversight has allowed teachers and administrators to amass costly prerequisites and to experiment with social engineering at taxpayer expense. Such "experimental" education has become increasingly expensive at a time when educational excellence as measured by the Scholastic Aptitude Tests has been falling. It may well be that the excessive "silliness" that passes for progressive education has impeded the instruction of American students.

Over the past 14 years, public spending on education has increased precipitously. In the same time span SAT scores have fallen steadily. If there is any correlation between spending and education quality it is a perverse one.

As a result of Proposition 13 and similar efforts in other states, the taxpayer will be a more zealous guardian of the public till, and parents will demand the elimination of frills and the pet projects of "professional educators."

A limit on spending such as that imposed by Proposition 13 forces greater responsiveness by school administrators to the interests of the parent/taxpayer. Such responsiveness will reduce the tax burden and provide American students with high quality education.

8
Appendices: Reference Section

Text of Proposition 13
Addition of Article XIII A to California State Constitution

Section 1. (a) the maximum amount of any ad valorem tax on real property shall not exceed One percent (1%) of the full cash value of such property. The one percent (1%) tax to be collected by the counties and apportioned according to law to the districts within the counties.

(b) The limitation provided for in subdivision (a) shall not apply to ad valorem taxes or special assessments to pay the interest and redemption charges on any indebtedness approved by the voters prior to the time this section becomes effective.

Section 2. (a) The full cash value means the County Assessors valuation of real property as shown on the 1975-76 tax bill under "full cash value," or thereafter, the appraised value of real property when purchased, newly constructed, or a change in ownership has occurred after the 1975 assessment. All real property not already assessed up to the 1975-76 tax levels may be reassessed to reflect that valuation.

(b) The fair market value base may reflect from year to year the inflationary rate not to exceed two percent (2%) for any given year or reduction as shown in the consumer price index or comparable data for the area under taxing jurisdiction.

Section 3. From and after the effective date of this article, any changes in State taxes enacted for the purpose of increasing revenues collected pursuant thereto whether by increased rates or changes in methods of computation must be imposed by an Act passed by not less than two-thirds of all members elected to each of the two houses of the Legislature, except that no new ad valorem taxes on real property, or sales or transaction taxes on the sales of real property may be imposed.

Section 4. Cities, Counties and special districts, by a two-thirds vote of the qualified electors of such district, may impose special taxes on such district, except ad valorem taxes on real property or a transaction tax or sales tax on the sale of real property within such City, County or special district.

Section 5. This article shall take effect for the tax year beginning on July 1 following the passage of this Amendment, except Section 3 which shall become effective upon the passage of this article.

Section 6. If any section, part, clause, or phrase hereof is for any reason held to be invalid or unconstitutional, the remaining sections shall not be affected but will remain in full force and effect.

Oregon
Proposal Limiting Ad Valorem
Property Taxes

Section 1. (a) The maximum amount of any ad valorem tax on real property shall not exceed One and one-half percent (1½%) of the full cash value of such property. The one and one-half percent (1½%) tax to be collected by the counties and apportioned according to law to the districts within the counties.

(b) The limitation provided for in subdivision (a) shall not apply to ad valorem taxes or special assessments to pay the interest and redemption charges on any indebtedness approved by the voters prior to the time this section becomes effective.

Section 2. (a) The full cash value means the County Assessors valuation of real property as shown on the 1975-76 tax bill under "full cash value"; or thereafter, the appraised value of real property when purchased, newly constructed, or a change in ownership has occured after the 1975 assessment. All real property not already assessed up to the 1975-76 tax levels may be reassessed to reflect that valuation.

(b) The Fair market value base may reflect from year to year the inflationary rate not to exceed two percent (2%) for any given year or reduction as shown in the consumer price index or comparable data for the area under taxing jurisdiction.

Section 3. From and after the effective date of this article, any changes in State taxes enacted for the purpose of increasing revenues collected pursuant thereto whether by increased rates or changes in methods of computation must be imposed by an Act passed by not less than two-thirds of all members elected to each of the two houses of the Legislature except that no new ad valorem taxes on real property, or sales or transaction taxes on the sales of real property may be imposed.

Section 4. Cities, Counties and special districts, by a two-thirds vote of the qualified electors of such district, may impose special taxes on such district, except ad valorem taxes on real property or a transaction tax or sales tax on the sale of real property within such City, County or special district.

Section 5. This article shall take effect for the tax year beginning on July 1 following the passage of this Amendment, except Section 3 which shall become effective upon the passage of this article.

Section 6. If any section, part, clause, or phrase hereof is for any reason held to be invalid or unconstitutional, the remaining sections shall not be affected but will remain in full force and effect.

Per Capita Revenue and Taxes Collected by State and Local Governments, by State, 1975-76

State	Total Revenue	Total Taxes	Property Taxes	Other Taxes	State	Total Revenue	Total Taxes	Property Taxes	Other Taxes
United States Average	$1,193.41	$730.52	$265.54	$464.98	Mississippi	958.98	486.19	109.59	376.60
Median State	1,141.49	671.41	235.90	423.03	Missouri	933.32	570.20	194.87	375.33
					Montana	1,292.22	708.88	350.25	358.62
Alabama	916.39	455.19	57.37	397.82	Nebraska	1,118.16	657.62	318.78	338.85
Alaska	3,349.04	1,895.84	1,048.12	847.72	Nevada	1,407.58	820.32	272.02	548.29
Arizona	1,141.49	731.43	282.18	449.25	New Hampshire	951.50	571.44	347.91	223.54
Arkansas	889.65	453.74	101.20	352.54	New Jersey	1,174.68	792.83	446.48	346.35
California	1,477.76	964.20	415.23	548.97	New Mexico	1,217.65	598.12	102.51	495.61
Colorado	1,266.07	728.00	271.29	456.71	New York	1,728.77	1,139.94	411.79	728.15
Connecticut	1,120.16	777.84	368.93	408.91	North Carolina	891.76	527.26	130.19	397.07
Delaware	1,372.09	768.30	130.12	638.18	North Dakota	1,295.87	666.91	212.28	454.63
D.C.	2,282.62	924.05	209.50	714.55	Ohio	967.87	585.79	223.65	362.15
Florida	963.78	565.80	191.36	374.44	Oklahoma	991.61	529.75	123.84	405.91
Georgia	1,002.28	548.65	177.94	370.72	Oregon	1,315.45	703.39	332.95	370.44
Hawaii	1,609.66	934.68	173.52	761.16	Pennsylvania	1,073.58	683.91	175.62	508.29
Idaho	1,075.82	590.38	190.12	400.26	Rhode Island	1,208.84	710.52	294.14	416.38
Illinois	1,160.55	769.42	283.95	485.46	South Carolina	927.68	489.20	115.76	373.44
Indiana	944.86	588.14	225.88	362.26	South Dakota	1,112.83	596.32	288.08	308.24
Iowa	1,156.12	700.64	277.60	423.03	Tennessee	905.27	493.17	129.49	363.67
Kansas	1,072.84	651.27	274.06	377.21	Texas	991.11	581.29	213.18	368.12
Kentucky	981.83	548.66	104.74	444.61	Utah	1,108.09	592.56	171.65	420.92
Louisiana	1,147.65	609.84	90.26	519.59	Vermont	1,323.57	742.00	307.88	434.11
Maine	1,094.20	671.42	297.01	374.41	Virginia	1,007.70	609.19	172.63	436.56
Maryland	1,293.40	814.25	239.36	574.89	Washington	1,256.12	728.00	235.91	492.10
Massachusetts	1,345.48	902.71	430.52	472.19	West Virginia	1,054.03	584.09	105.96	478.13
Michigan	1,273.51	749.04	324.22	424.82	Wisconsin	1,262.84	790.57	288.60	501.97
Minnesota	1,362.15	822.68	254.20	568.47	Wyoming	1,684.37	846.56	351.61	494.95

Source: U.S. Department of Commerce, Bureau of the Census, *Governmental Finances in 1975-76*

Public School Enrollments and Average Per-Pupil Expenditures by State, 1976-1977

State or Other Area	Enrollment (thousands)	Per-Pupil Expenditures	State or Other Area	Enrollment (thousands)	Per-Pupil Expenditures
Alabama	759	$1,163	Nebraska	316	1,534
Alaska	89	2,938	Nevada	140	1,423
Arizona	493	1,446	New Hampshire	175	1,261
Arkansas	457	1,112	New Jersey	1,458	2,104
California	4,420	1,595	New Mexico	275	1,354
Colorado	569	1,556	New York	3,401	2,333
Connecticut	652	1,888	North Carolina	1,185	1,210
Delaware	127	1,875	North Dakota	131	1,391
District of Columbia	130	2,060	Ohio	2,293	1,403
Florida	1,551	1,483	Oklahoma	595	1,261
Georgia	1,090	1,187	Oregon	478	1,600
Hawaii	176	1,689	Pennsylvania	2,246	1,862
Idaho	197	1,158	Rhode Island	176	1,551
Illinois	2,270	1,876	South Carolina	630	1,208
Indiana	1,226	1,269	South Dakota	151	1,280
Iowa	612	1,669	Tennessee	877	1,146
Kansas	448	1,510	Texas	2,813	1,154
Kentucky	692	1,155	Utah	310	1,243
Louisiana	847	1,248	Vermont	105	1,440
Maine	251	1,333	Virginia	1,104	1,368
Maryland	881	1,659	Washington	785	1,694
Massachusetts	1,198	1,992	West Virginia	404	1,194
Michigan	2,073	1,737	Wisconsin	964	1,743
Minnesota	880	1,777	Wyoming	88	1,749
Mississippi	512	1,072			
Missouri	965	1,300	U.S. Total	44,300	1,578
Montana	172	1,755			

Source: U.S. Department of Health, Education and Welfare, National Center for Education Statistics

Index of Names

130